CHAUCER'S VERSE

CHAUCER'S VERSE

Paull F. Baum

DUKE UNIVERSITY PRESS · DURHAM, N. C. · 1961

THIS BOOK IS PUBLISHED WITH
THE ASSISTANCE OF A GRANT
FROM THE RESEARCH COUNCIL
OF DUKE UNIVERSITY AND A
GRANT TO THE DUKE UNIVERSITY
PRESS BY THE FORD FOUNDATION

PREFACE

For the last fifty years or more there has been no attempt to examine the whole subject of Chaucer's meters, to ascertain what may have been his principles of versification and how clearly he followed them and to what effect. Now, however, that we have better texts than the earlier scholars had, it should be possible to make some progress and by deductive methods to come reasonably close to an appreciation of his verse and its rhythms.

Such a study faces two difficulties. One is the confusion which exists among specialists in versification and rhythm, their often recondite terminology, and their frequent disagreements among themselves—all of which have made the subject repellent and needlessly obscure to non-specialists. The other is the difficulty which inheres in the study of a language whose sounds are unfamiliar to modern ears. I have, therefore, used only the simplest and commonest terms and avoided, so far as possible, all controversial matter—except one, which I have relegated to an appendix.

P.F.B.

CONTENTS

CHAUCER'S VERSE

CHAPTER I. METER

1. INTRODUCTION

THE earliest comments on Chaucer's versification are mainly of historical or curious interest, but there were a few exceptions. Gascoigne as early as 1575 recognized prophetically one of the chief problems: "Also our father *Chaucer* hath vsed the same libertie in feete and measures that the Latinists do vse: and who so euer do peruse and well consider his workes, he shall finde that although his lines are not alwayes of one selfe same number of Syllables, yet beyng redde by one that hath vnderstanding. . . ."[1] Speght also in his second edition of *The Workes*, 1602, took much the same view:

And for his verses, although in diuers places they seeme to vs to stand of vnequal measures: yet a skilfull Reader, that can scan them in their nature, shall find it otherwise. And if a verse here and there fal out a sillable shorter or longer than another, I rather aret it to the negligence and rape of *Adam Scrivener*, that I may speake as Chaucer doth, than to any vnconning or ouersight in the Author. . . .

Dryden's "the rude Sweetness of a *Scotch* Tune" (1700) is familiar. Then gradually the value of *-e* and syllabic endings came to be recognized. Thomas Morell could say in the Preface to his edition of the *Canterbury Tales* (1737), apropos of *faile in a sillable* (HF 1098):

From this last Line, I conclude, that an exact Numerosity (as Bp. *Sprat* expresses it in his Life of Cowley . . .) was not *Chaucer's* main Care; but that he had sometimes a greater Regard for the Sense than the Metre; His Numbers however, are, by no Means so rough and inharmonious as some People imagine; there is a charming Simplicity in them, and they are always musical, whether they want or exceed their Complement. . . .

And as to final *-e*, says Morell, "our Author seems to have taken the Liberty to use it or not, as it best suited his Metre."

During the last hundred years there has been real progress.

1. *Certayne Notes of Instruction concerning the making of verse or rime in English.*

Child's *Observations* came in 1862; Ellis' *On Early English Pronunciation* in 1867-1888; Schipper's *Englische Metrik* in 1881-1888 (condensed and revised as *Grundriss der Englischen Metrik*, 1895); and ten Brink's *Chaucers Sprache und Verskunst* in 1884 (English translation 1891; third edition 1920); and then a few pages by Skeat, a syllabic rigorist, in vol. vi of the Oxford Chaucer, 1894. Several general works on English versification have remarks on Chaucer, including Saintsbury's, fluent as always and crotchety. Miss Hammond's *Bibliographical Manual* (1908) has several pages (481-502) with many acute and sensible observations; but she was obliged to say: "we have not yet made that thorough and unbiased examination of the texts which alone will enable us to say what variants Chaucer permitted himself on the analogy of the substituted anapest in Tennyson or the wrenched accent so frequent in Swinburne." By now, however, most of the texts (except for the Minor Poems) seem to be as near definition as we are likely to come and it is time for a fresh start.

What we should most like to have is some pronouncement, some indication, or at the least, some hints, from the poet about his theory and his practice in the writing of verse. And we have none—almost none. For example, our word *rhythm* did not exist for him.[2] In the introduction to MLT it is said jokingly

> *That Chaucer though he kan but lewedly*
> *On metres and on ryming craftily.* B 47-48

In the Monk's Prologue the Monk, preparing the audience for his hundred tragedies, explains that commonly tragedies are composed in hexameter, some also in prose,

> *And eke in metre in many a sondry wyse,* B 3171

almost as though hexameter was not a meter. But the general term is used more sensibly at the end of the F Prologue (not in the G Prologue) to LGW, where the God of Love says to the poet:

2. The earliest citation in NED is c1557; even then it is hard to distinguish from rime.

Make the metres of hem as the leste,   F 562

that is, for the Legends he may choose whatever metrical form
he likes. This of course is a bit of fooling, inasmuch as they
are all, like the Prologue, in five-stress couplets; and is probably,
as Kittredge noted, an echo in reverse of the injunction which
the King of Navarre lays upon Machaut in *Le jugement dou Roy
de Navarre.*[3]

The word *rime* (noun and verb) occurs some thirty times,
usually in the sense of writing or speaking in verse (so also
rymeyed F 711): twice with *endyte* (PF 119, HF 520), once in
contrast (?) to *cadence* (HF 623), and three times in contrast
to prose (B 96, LGW F 66, Scogan 41). In B 1899 the Sir Thopas
is called a *rym*, but the Host labels it *rym dogerel* (B 2115)—
disapprovingly. But twice Chaucer uses it in the stricter sense of
similar sounds: in the Compleynt of Venus 80:

Syth rym in Englissh hath such skarsete,

and apparently in *Troilus* III 90: *as I may my rymes holde.* And
in I 44 the Parson contrasts it with alliteration—*rom ram ruf.*

The word *verse* may signify (*a*) meter in general: Ovid
wrote Medea's *lettre in verse* (LGW 1678); (*b*) a line of verse:
in BD the Knight makes a song of ten or twelve verses; so also
in HF 1098 *som vers*, in B 4503 the *vers* of Dan Burnel the Ass,
in Melibeus B 2295-2300, 2800-2805, and in *Loo, next this vers, Tr.*
I 399; (*c*) a stanza: Litel Clergeon memorized the first stanza of
Alma Redemptoris, B 1712; and (*d*) either a line or a stanza:
The nexte vers (PF 679), *Thise woful vers* (*Tr.* I 7).

One word has baffled nearly everyone. In HF the Eagle,
promising the poet some reward for his hitherto ill-founded
writing about Love, reminds him that he has applied what
little *wit* he has

    To make bookys, songes, dytees,
    In ryme, or elles in cadence.   HF 622-23

(This word occurs nowhere else in Chaucer. Gower has, *Confessio
Amantis* IV, 2414,

3. *MPh* VII (1910), 471-74. There are similar injunctions elsewhere in
French which Chaucer may or may not have seen.

Of metre, of rime, and of cadence.)

Robinson suggests that a contrast is intended and that the most likely contrast is that with unrimed alliterative verse, or possibly prose. But Chaucer, so far as we know, wrote nothing in *reverence Of Love* either in alliterative verse or in prose.[4] The word later means rhythm. Professor Southworth has "What Chaucer himself calls verses of cadence" (p. 36; cf. also p. 65); and on p. 52 he suggests glossing *or elles* as 'otherwise,' rather against his own argument for the sense of non-metrical rhythm. (On Southworth cf. pp. 117 ff. below.) This last however seems to fit best: 'in rime, or you might call it cadence, from the fall of the voice at the end of a line.' This agrees with the musical use, though in mediæval music the term was *clausula*. In any case Chaucer's Eagle was speaking lightly and he may have meant no more than 'in rime or meter.'

This is little enough, and hardly goes beyond vocabulary.

In the Invocation to Book III of HF Chaucer disclaims any show of *maistrye* or of *art poetical*,

> *But for the rym ys lyght and lewed,*
> *Yit make hyt sumwhat agreable,*
> *Though som vers fayle in a sillable.*   HF 1096-98

This last line has been misunderstood. Skeat took it to mean simply that some lines had only seven instead of the expected eight syllables. Robinson says, more cautiously, that it "seems to be a definite acknowledgment on Chaucer's part of his practice of writing verses without the full number of syllables," that is, seven in the short couplet, nine in the longer line; then he adds: "Or is it simply a prayer for indulgence with imperfect verses?" The word *rym* stands for the whole poem, or specifically the *lytel laste bok*; which is *lyght and lewed* enough, although tedious in parts. Nor is it in Book III that Chaucer begins to employ seven-syllable lines. The real question turns on

4. Hope Emily Allen, "Mystical Lyrics of the *Manuel des Pechiez*," *RR* IX (1918), 154-93, quotes p. 187 a passage from the *Manuel* in which "cadence" clearly signifies rhythmic or even poetic prose and in n. 75 says of Chaucer's line that the word "could in this sense be well applied to the *Boethius*." But the Eagle could hardly have had Chaucer's Boece in mind.

fayle in a sillable. Now Chaucer's idiom is regularly fail *of* when the sense is to lack, be wanting in:

> *That he wolde hir of trouthe fayle;*   HF 297

to *failen of his praye* ABC 64; *Of silver . . . shaltow nat faille* B 1438 (also 1465); *faille of his conclusion* D 430; etc. His only apparent example of fail with *in* is Bo IV, p. 4, 1400-1405 (Robinson l. 270, p. 366): *fayle and cesen in al*, i.e., in respect to everything. There can thus be hardly a doubt that here in HF 1098 Chaucer means that some syllable in a line may here and there be not altogether right, metrically; in short (as Robinson would not quite say), some of the lines may be rough. And this is wholly consistent with the context. In fact, Chaucer therewith illustrates his point by forcing the metrical stress on *a* and on the suffix *-able*. The greatest error would be to take the phrase as implying that Chaucer's practice was to measure his lines by the number of syllables.

More fruitful may be a look at the possible sources of Chaucer's knowledge of versification. He had read some of the rhetoricians, but they had little to tell him about metrics.[5] He had read no doubt observantly the French poets themselves, to see how they worked, and after 1372 the Italian poets Boccaccio and Dante, and some of Petrarch. He may have discussed the subject with his friend Gower—if so, would that we had some record. Certainly he must have recognized that the two languages were different from English; and it is highly improbable that he had ever heard an Italian read his poetry aloud.

The development of early French versification from the quantitative measures of classical Latin through the later accentual Latin verse has often been traced, and most recently and fully

5. In November 1392 (too late to have helped Chaucer) Deschamps composed at the command of "son seigneur" his *L'Art de dictier et de fere chançons, balades, virelais et rondeaux* (*SATF* XI, 115-21). Here versification is not a branch of rhetoric but of music. Some of the directions are minute, others quite general, and the whole both incomplete (in the MSS) and confused. No source is known, but since Deschamps drew his examples from his own poems the little treatise would seem to be a codification of his own practice.

by M. Lote.[6] It is a complex history with still many uncertainties. Early discussions, before the fifteenth century are rare, but by the thirteenth century the principle of syllabism was well established.[7] From Dante's master, Brunetto Latini, we have: "Car qui bien voudra rimer, il li convient conter totes les sillabes . . ."; but this must be qualified by the statement of P. Febre: "Rithme n'est aultre chose que langaige mesurè par longueur de syllabes en conveniente termination, proporcionallement accentué."[8] Dante simply says, as taken for granted, that lines of verse are measured by syllables, varying from three to eleven in number, with the eleven-syllable line the stateliest—as in his *Commedia—videtur esse superbius, tam temporis occupatione, quam capacite sententiae, constructionis, et vocabulorum.*[9]

None the less, syllabism was never all. From that moment, however gradual it was in coming, when the new French language ceased to hear itself spoken with a distinct lexical accent, as the Latin was spoken, there was nothing for it but to count syllables as a measure of verse. At the same time it was necessary for the poets to recognize some sort of stress in the use of rime (or assonance) and also at caesural pauses. Little as is certainly known now about the sound of mediæval French verse, and variable as are the effects of syllabic emphasis in modern French verse, it is at least clear that while the count of syllables was the chief determinant, other considerations entered into the making and delivery of verse. Much the same is true of Italian, though the spoken language is accentual, with a stronger admixture than in English of variations of pitch. The fact is, and it is so recognized

6. Georges Lote, *Histoire du vers français.* I, Première Partie: Le Moyen Age, Paris, 1949.

7. Long before this Bede, in his *De Arte metrica,* had distinguished between *rhythmus* and meter as "verborum modulata compositio non metrica ratione, sed numero syllabarum ad judicium aurium examinata, ut sunt carmina vulgarium poetarum" (MSL 90, 173).

8. Lote, p. 292. Little is known of Pierre le Febre of Rouen. He died before 1521 and his *Le. grand et vray Art de pleine rhétorique* enjoyed six editions between 1521 and 1544.

9. *De Vulgari Eloquentia* II, v. This could not be bettered for clearness. Chaucer felt the same, for only twice did he use the octosyllabic or four-stress line; or three times, including Sir Thopas.

in the face of theory, that some of the elements of a prosody of stress are present in French and Italian verse, presumably also in the fourteenth century as later; and therefore, for Chaucer's ear, accustomed to a speech with well marked lexical accent, both principles would operate together. The blend—or call it compromise—would be easy and natural. M. Legouis has described the situation clearly:

> C'est chose significative que dès le moyen âge, dans le milieu anglais, les vers en langue française ou anglo-normande qui se sont écrits, ont tendu de bonne heure à régulariser et balancer leurs accents. Comme ce n'est pas l'alexandrin qui était alors en usage mais le vers de huit ou de dix syllabes, c'est vers un mouvement iambique qu'on les a vus alors s'acheminer. Ils ont insensiblement changé de nature. On le sent très bien dans Gower:
>
> > Le mois de maij sest en yvern mué,
> > Lurtie truis si je la Rose quière,
> > Vous estes franche et jeo sui fort lié.
>
> On peut de même imaginer l'allure que prenait en entrant dans la ballade de Chaucer (*Fortune*) notre décasyllabe encadré de vers héroïques au rhythme nettement iambique:
>
> > Jay tout perdu, mon temps et mon labour.[10]

As Gower, an Englishman writing in French, so Chaucer. Whatever the movement to a Frenchman writing French verse, for an Englishman reading it the movement became naturally, inevitably iambic.[11]

The situation may be restated more emphatically. The language which Chaucer used, which he spoke and heard, was a Germanic language with definite lexical accent; and when he composed in verse his language was still the same. When he read his poems to himself and when he recited them aloud to others, it was still the language of his normal speech adapted to metrical patterns as he understood them. How he read the verse of his contemporary French poets we can only guess. We must assume that he was aware of its syllabism, but it does not follow that he

10. Emile Legouis, *Défense de la Poésie. Française*, Paris and London, 1912, pp. 82-83.

11. It may not be relevant but it is true that we to-day reading mediæval French poetry find no difficulty in making it go to an iambic rhythm; or rather, we find difficulty in making it go otherwise.

adopted it as his prime metrical principle; and if he had tried, even so his ear would not have been satisfied with making a line of verse out of just only ten syllables. The syllables would have to afford a recognizable series of repeated units determined by the conventional accents of his words—an iambic pattern, te-tum te-tum, varied by all the devices of unequal stress, of pause and time values, of phrasal and syntactic patterns, that he could find.

Miss Hammond took a different view, which deserves consideration.

Far from regarding Chaucer's line, with Schipper, as the descendant of the Old English bipartite, heavily stressed verse; far from regarding it as akin to the French syllable-counting movement; far even from regarding it as the struggle and compromise of these two systems, I would see in Boccaccio and in Dante the true instructors of Chaucer. The briefest dip into Boccaccio's Filostrato will reveal the overrunning lines and the varying length of phrase which we class among Chaucer's most admirable freedoms, will show us the reversal of rhythm (or substituted trochee), and the skilful use of rhythmic emphasis to support idea-emphasis. Compare for instance Chaucer's rendition of

> Tu savio, tu amico, tu sai tutto   Filostr. II, st. 33

into

> But thou wys, thou wost, thou mayst, thou art al   Troilus I: 1052

and observe his recognition and accentuation of the Italian's stresses.

Miss Hammond compares also *Filostrato* III, st. 78 with *Troilus* III 302 ff., where the verbs are held over to begin a new line: *Tien* and *Seyd*; and she continues:

there can be little question but that he learned from the great Italians the essentials of his art. Could he fail to perceive, at the opening of the Inferno, the effect of the double reversal of stress in

> Questa selva selvaggia ed aspra e forte?

Could it escape him that his translation

> The day gan feilen, and the derke night   PoFoules 85

followed with fidelity the movement of Dante's

> Lo giorno andava, e l'aer bruno?

Perhaps these are rhetorical questions. For in her very next words Miss Hammond gives her case away by conceding that Chaucer's verse is necessarily "more strongly accentual" than the Italian.

"Indeed, it is a question if, with all his knowledge of Italian poetry, Chaucer did not grasp it more by eye than by ear. . . ."[12] Indeed, it is still a question how great was his knowledge of Italian poetry—enough to follow Boccaccio and to lift phrases from Dante, granted—but how can one argue the influence of the sound of Italian verse on his without knowing more than we know of how it sounded to him?

But finally now, however he may have come to it, Chaucer's line is a series of five iambs.[13] For this line he had no native models—though a few isolated specimens have been turned up— and the means of relieving monotony he either discovered for himself or deduced intuitively from foreign models. One thing may be said with security, that modern English versification starts with Chaucer. With him it was almost a *de novo* creation. He found and used nearly all the liberties and the methods of obtaining variety which later poets have employed in the five-stress iambic line; yet not quite all, for it stands to reason that dramatic blank verse and certain forms of the lyric were outside his ken and his practice. Alexandrines cannot be established in his verse and he never tried the free mixture of iamb and anapest which distinguishes much of Swinburne's verse. Whether he both composed in iambics and counted syllables is a question to be re-served for later, with only the passing note that five iambs regularly make ten syllables.

Here a warning is necessary. The text of Chaucer is at all times a hazard for the prosodist. Great gains have been made in recent times, but one must still walk cautiously. It would be too painful, however, to hesitate over every line and often I have

12. *Manual*, pp. 486-87.

13. For this flat statement there is to be sure only deductive evidence. If it must be regarded as in the first instance an assumption or an hypothesis, it can be tested in the usual ways of corroboration and accounting for ap-parent exceptions. Furthermore, if the Popper principle is invoked—namely that an hypothesis is validated not by the number of corroborative details but by the number and variety of attempts to falsify it—one may refer to Appendix 1 below on what I have called The Rhythmical or Four-Beat Heresy. See Karl R. Popper, *The Logic of Scientific Discovery*, London, 1958.

passed over the variants when there seemed to be no question of
meter. For the *Canterbury Tales* I have used the text of Manly and
Rickert, with due reserve and with attention to all the scribal
variations. For the *Troilus* I have used Root, chiefly because his
apparatus is fuller than Robinson's, although his preference for
β over γ may be a mistake. For BD and HF and LGW and for
the Minor Poems I have used Robinson's text, second edition;
that of Koch is too cluttered with emendation. The Chaucerian
Romaunt is textually so unsatisfactory that I have avoided it,
perhaps unwisely.

As an illustration of some of the problems one fairly simple
case may serve. In *Tr.* II 795-97 both Root and Robinson read

> *Or wher bycometh it, whan it is ago.*
> *Ther is no wight that woot, I trowe so,*
> *Wher it bycometh; lo, no wight on it sporneth.*

Robinson submits no variants. According to Root
for *bycometh* in 795 JClSı have *becomth*;
for *whan* CpHıSıGgR have *whan that;*
ago is the reading of CpHıJAH5; H2 Cx have *gone;* the rest
                                    (ClH3H4HıPhRSıS2Th) have *go.*
Of these the *gone* of H2Cx may be dismissed because of the rime.
For *bycometh* in 797 J has *becomth.* Now *bycometh* in 795 may
have two syllables or three depending on the rest of the line, but
in 797 surely, if the syllable count is held to ten, it must be
read as disyllabic, though it is cumbersome to pronounce so and
contrasts with *sporneth*, which presumably is not reduced to
spornth. Only J however reads *becomth* in 797. One cannot argue
that if it is a disyllable in 797 it is the same in 795, for Chaucer
is not always consistent. Yet, again counting syllables, it looks as
though *bycometh* in 795 must be a disyllable and JClSı are right
with *becomth*, and J is right, in both cases. Only the editors are
wrong if they expect a reader to be guided by their spelling—
except Globe, which prints *becom'th* in both lines.

For the rest of 795 there is a choice between *whan* and *whan
that*, and the authorities are divided: CpHı being for *whan that*
and ClJ for *whan.* There is also a choice between *ago* and *go* and

the authorities are divided differently: CpH1J for *ago,* but ClH4
(and a dozen more) for *go.* What have the editors done? Both
Root and Robinson took Cp, a γ ms, as the basis of their text—
Robinson adding Cl and H1 (also γ) and Root adding J (here
β) as containing Chaucer's final revision. In this case Root had
no option; his bases are for *ago.* But Robinson had to opt between
Cp and Cl and he chose Cp.

The situation may be put more simply, waiving secondary
MSS:

Or wher bycometh it whan it is ago	Cp
Or wher becomth it whan it is go	Cl
Or wher becomth it whan it is ago	J

Of these Cp appears to have an extra syllable; Cl to be short one
syllable, unless *becomth* is expanded to three syllables; and J
looks like the best text and might well have been Root's choice
for the whole line. Robinson, on the other hand, is partly Cp
and partly Cl. When all is said, the line is not a very good one;
but we are still in doubt just what Chaucer wrote or how he
meant it to sound.[14]

2. THE FIVE-STRESS LINE

THE foregoing generalizations may best be illustrated by a
trial analysis of the Compleynt unto Pite (P) as a specimen
of Chaucer's very early practice compared with the first hundred
lines of the General Prologue (A) as a specimen of his later
and most mature versification. In these two passages will be
found nearly all the metrical variations, nearly all the liberties
and licenses, which occur elsewhere; namely (1) the weak stress,
including secondary accent in polysyllables, in different positions
in the line; (2) the heavy foot or spondee; (3) the inverted foot or
trochaic substitution; (4) the variable use of syllabic *e;* and (5)
elision, contraction, and the slurs which may or may not certify

14. Other examples of textual difficulties are noted *passim.*

the admission or exclusion of trisyllabic feet. The last two of these, however, as being the most difficult, will be held over until pp. 17 ff.

Both P and A have a normal or expected proportion of regular iambic lines:

With herte soore, and ful of besy peyne	P 2
That slepen al the nyght with open eye.	A 10

Both have a weak stress in the first foot:

That in this world was never wight so woo	P 3
Upon the crueltee and tirannye	P 6
And for the soule I shop me for to preye	P 20
That hem hath holpen whan that they were seeke	A 18
For he was late ycome from his viage	A 77
Of his stature he was of euene lengthe.	A 83

Both show a weak stress in the second foot:

My purpos was to Pite to compleyne	P 5
Of Love, that for my trouthe doth me dye	P 7
Sheweth unto youre rial excellence	P 59
And palmeres for to seken straunge strondes	A 13
And specially from euery shires ende.	A 15

Both show a weak stress in the third foot:

Withoute dethe,—and, yf I shal not feyne	P 4
Or tellen any of my peynes smarte	P 13
So many men as in her tyme hir knewe	P 31
The tendre croppes and the yonge sonne	A 7
Wel nyne and twenty in a compaignye	A 24
Er that I ferther in this tale pace.	A 36

Both show a weak stress in the fourth foot:

My purpos was, to Pite to compleyne	P 5
I fond hir ded, and buried in an herte	P 14
And for the soule I shop me for to preye	P 20

The droghte of March hath perced to the roote   A 2
Of which vertu engendered is the flour   A 4
So priketh hem nature in hir corages   A 11
In Southwerk at the Tabard as I lay.   A 20

Similarly the fifth foot may often be or seem weak when the
line ends in a polysyllable and a secondary accent must do for
the stress: *tirannye* P 6, *sodeynly* P 32, *besely* P 33; *pilgrymages* A
12, *hostelrye* A 23, *compaignye* A 24.

The examples cited are merely illustrative. Often there are
two weak stresses in the same line—more often perhaps in
Chaucer than in later poets—and the line may therefore seem
empty; yet not always, for by such means emphasis is laid on
the principal words, as in

The chambres and the stables weren wyde   A 28
And wel we weren esed atte beste.   A 29

This practice is so common in Chaucer as to amount to a characteristic. Much depends however on the context and on the
degree of stress given to the light syllable. For example, in the
lines just quoted *Er* A 36 comes nearer to deserving full stress
than *his* A 83, *hem* A 18 than *for* A 13; and so on. In A 7 *and*
is not really stressed at all; the pause after *croppes* covers up or
compensates for the expected stress. Similarly, and most often in
the fourth place, as in *buried in an herte* P 14, *Perced to the roote*
A 2, though there is no pause, the assumed emphasis on *in* and *to*
is partly disguised by the phrasal formula and partly due to the
meaning of the verbs. But this is not true of the expected stress
on the second *for* P 20, where it is a concession to meter.

Spondaic effects. Although spondees in the classical sense do
not occur in English verse, the term is convenient to describe
examples in which a theoretically light syllable for one reason or
another (usually rhetorical emphasis) is stronger than strict meter
requires.

In ydel hope, folk redeless of peyne   P 27
That no wight woot that she is ded, but I   P 30

> *Than longen folk to goon on pilgrymages*   A 12
> *Wel nyne and twenty in a compaignye.*   A 24

A somewhat similar effect is produced by inversion, as in

> *In lystes thries and ay slayn his foo.*   A 63

Inverted foot, trochaic substitution. Neither of these terms is quite satisfactory because they seem to imply that the rhythm is reversed; but since they are conventional they are used here. Inversion serves for emphasis and for variety, but in Chaucer's practice it seems often a mere convenience.

Inversion is particularly frequent in the first foot and helps to disguise a weak stress:

> *Kepynge the corps, as ye have herd me seyn*   P 51
> *Sheweth unto youre rial excellence*   P 59
> *Thus for your deth I may wel wepe and pleyne*   P 118

> *Redy to wenden on my pilgrymage*   A 21
> *So hadde I spoken with hem euerichon*   A 31
> *Syngyne he was or floytynge al the day.*   A 91

Inversion is less common in the second place and is there likely to follow a trochee in the first foot:

> *Let som strem of youre lyght on me be sene*   P 94
> *Al bismotered with his habergeoun.*   A 76

In the third foot inversion often follows a pause:
> *Adoun I fel when that I saugh the herse*   P 15
> *Ded as a stoon, while that the swogh me laste*   P 16
> *Humblest of herte, highest of reverence*   P 57

> *Whan Zephirus eek with his sweete breeth*   A 5
> *To telle yow al the condicioun*   A 38
> *Of ech of hem so as it semed me*   A 39

In the fourth foot inversion has a peculiar effect, coming so far along in the line. Often it serves to disguise or compensate for a weak stress.

> *What maner man dar now holde up his heed*   P 24
> *Your renoun ys fordoo than in a throwe*   P 86

At Alisaundre he was whan it was wonne   A 51
In Gernade at the seege eek hadde he be.   A 56

Inversion of the fifth foot is rare at all periods. It occurs in Chaucer only when he forces the stress, for rime, on an ordinarily unaccented syllable: *redý ladý, worthí,* etc. (See below pp. 31, 36.) Somewhat similar is his riming of normally unaccented *-esse* and *-ynge* (when not a secondary accent). There is no example in Pite, but the equally early ABC has *distresse humblesse maistresse goodnesse* 106-11 (also 138-43),—where the first three words, of French origin, may get some stress on the suffix, but *goodnesse* is different—and *woninge bringe* 145/47. In the General Prologue the first examples are *wynnyng thing* A 275/76 (also 325/26) and *fairnesse bisynesse* 519/20; but they are common enough elsewhere. See below pp. 34-36.

The purpose of the foregoing paragraphs—still leaving the problems of *e* and of elision etc.—is merely to show that from the very beginning, say 1369 or 1370, the elemental structure of Chaucer's five-stress iambic line is that which remained his staple. He learned at once to play the instrument. Later he would learn to get a finer music from it.

It is very difficult to discuss syllabic *e* systematically because the poet himself was inconsistent. Superficially this *e* is of two sorts: historical, i.e., either inflectional or descended from an unaccented vowel in the earlier form of the language or in French loan words; and scribal, i.e., an *-e* more or less gratuitously added (or omitted) by the fifteenth-century copyists and more or less carefully adjusted by modern editors. By apocope we get *maner* for *manere.* By syncope we get *werde* for *werede*; both *seyst* and *seyest,* both *comth* and *cometh.* Contractions like *maad* for *makede, kid* for *kythed, clad* for *clothed, rit* for *rideth, bind* for *bindeth,* etc. were already established and could be used as alternative forms. The same is true of *eek,* for which Chaucer has occasionally *eke* in rime; and of the feminine pronominal adjective *hir,* which in rime may be *hire, here.* And so on. The manuscripts are not to be trusted and perhaps Chaucer had not been too careful to make distinctions in his holograph. His words to Adam on his copying of the *Troilus* reveal his concern for details,

but between his original and our copies there are too many missing
links to let us reason with confidence. It goes without saying that
Chaucer took every advantage of all these choices, leaving the
reader sometimes in doubt, often to decide (or even to emend)
according to the scansion. Moreover, having grown up in London,
where he heard many dialectal forms from other parts of England,
Chaucer had available another kind of choice for metrical convenience and for rimes.[1] See p. 38 below.

The simplest statement would be that Chaucer's use of *-e*
within the line is "facultative," "a technical poetic [*sc.* metrical]
device," in other words a convenience. Like the rainbow it comes
and goes, and when it crossed the formal iambic pattern it is,
or may be, heard so lightly—*unnethe it mighte be lesse*—that it
does not upset the rhythm. This is the commonly accepted view;
both Donaldson and Southworth agree on it, though the latter
with reservations of his own. For example *haddě he* A 386,
haddę he A 392; *namęly* A 1675, *namely* A 1877;

> *Theras by auenture this Palamoun*   A 1516
> *Of auenturě happed hir to meete*   F 1501

(note hiatus where elision might be expected).

> *Short was his gowne with sleues longe and wyde*   A 93

(where the *-e* of *longe* disappears by elision, but that of *gowne*,
before the pause, might well be sounded). A rather special instance is

> *But soore wepte she if oon of hem were deed.*   A 148

If the *-e* of *soore, wepte,* and *were* is pronounced the line becomes
an alexandrine, and was so taken by Ellis, but rejected by Schip-

1. The ways of language are not like the rules in a book. Developments
are gradual, uneven, irregular. It is likely that Chaucer used, for metrical
convenience, some dialectal forms which were not customary in his every-
day spoken language. For general discussion see B. ten Brink, *Chaucers
Sprache und Verskunst,* 1884, 1899 (Eng. transl., 1901), 1920, 256 ff.;
and for recent opinions J. G. Southworth, "Chaucer's Final *-e* in Rhyme,"
PMLA LXII (1947), 910-35 and E. Talbot Donaldson, "Chaucer's Final
-E," *ibid.* LXIII (1948), 1101-24, followed by expostulation and reply, *ibid.*
LXIV (1949), 601-10. Earlier discussions are for the most part invalidated
by faulty method or unsettled texts.

per, with a wrong explanation. Skeat has *weep* for *wepte* and took *she if oon* as one foot, *sh' if oon*. But there is no problem, though all three words may appear elsewhere as disyllables.

Elision is one of the chief trouble-makers. Manly's account of it may be taken as typical. "Final unstressed *e* was regularly elided in verse when followed by a word beginning with a vowel or a silent or lightly stressed *h*." Then he adds: "Elision is not confined to the vowel *e*," but may include the unstressed *o* in *to*, also sometimes the *o* in *so*. Further: "When the personal pronouns *I* and *thou* preceded an initial vowel the second vowel was probably dropped:

> *And slee me in this wode ther I am inne*   [A 1618]
> *But, for as muche thou art a worthy knight."*[2]   [A 1608]

The word "dropped" should be noted. Ten Brink, however, is more careful. Elision, he says (269) "comprehends all the diverse phenomena which result from the blending into one syllable of the final vowel of one word with the initial vowel of the next. They are principally of two kinds: ecthlepsis or apostrophe, and 'synklisis'. . . . Actual crasis is rare." A possible crasis is *they engendred* A 421. His synklisis is illustrated by *so besy a man* and *many a*; but cf. *many oon* (three syllables). Here the operative word is "blending."[3]

The question, thus, is whether the *-e* (or *-o*) is dropped, that is, suppressed in reading, silenced completely, or somehow blended with the following vowel, that is, presumably allowed a diminished, half-heard enunciation. The distinction is one between total absorption and smooth amalgamation. Metrically, for purposes of scansion, are there two syllables? or one syllable? or so to say one-and-a half—or less than two but more than one?

2. *Canterbury Tales*, New York, 1928, pp. 125-27. But in A 1618 it is surely more reasonable to scan *wode* as monosyllabic.

3. Skeat (VI, 67) gives three empirical rules, to which there may be exceptions. He is both clear and firm with "The cæsural pause prevents elision." In such words as *specially* he says the *i* blends with the following vowel; but in *Canterb'ry* for example the syllable is suppressed. "Blending" is not altogether a happy word. One cannot be sure of course, but perhaps the vowels united to form a kind of diphthong, in which each vowel preserves its values, one being subordinated to the other.

In single cases the difference may be set aside as unimportant, e.g., *the estaat, the array*, for which some scribes actually wrote *thestaat, tharray*; but when the preceding word is more emphatic or distinct than the mere article, one wonders, one hesitates; e.g., in *thee alighte* B 1660, where both the El and Hg scribes wrote *thalighte* (followed by Manly in print). There are many such cases—*do mendite* G 32 (Hg, Manly), *Pryvee and apert* D 1114, *Pitee exyled* Sted 17, *Tisbe and* LGW 916, *By eterne word* A 1109, *victorie and* A 872, 916, *Nero and of* A 2032, *peeple hath* E 993, *victorie of* A 1235, *wepne hast* A 1601, *wepne haue* A 1591. A quite remarkable example is

> *Thanne seyde he O cruel goddes that gouerne.*   A 1303

Two examples in the early ABC are worth noting: *Continue on us thi* 88, *an Ave-Marie or tweye* 104; and in Pite 11 *Cruelte me awreke* (*Cru'lte me awreke?* or *Cruelte m'awreke?*). Such examples are to be remembered as verging on if not actually amounting to the trisyllabic foot.

The various slurs present the same kind of uncertainty. Manageable are those with intervocalic *r*: *fader of* A 2469, *water he* A 400, *lever have* A 293, *over al* A 1207, and those with *-l-*: *candel at* D 334. Somewhat different, but frequent, is elision through *-n* (or perhaps better called syncope): *riden in* A 57, *writen a* A 161, *geten hym* A 261, *pynchen at* A 326, *weren up* A 455 (beside *werèn of* A 456), *risen and* A 1065, *riden anon* A 1628, etc., etc.; in some of these the *-n* may be scribal. Examples like *biloved and* A 215, *overloked hyt* BD 232 may be simple contractions. *Over, evere, nevere, hevene* are variable, sometimes monosyllabic, sometimes certainly disyllabic. Different again are such words as *positif* A 1167 and *Infinite* A 1259, which for purposes of scansion are apparently disyllabic. One might compile a list of examples ranging from natural and easy to possible, probable, and improbable.[4]

4. One concession to law and order was made by those who held with the caesura heresy, brought over from classical metrics. When there is a true pause, and even sometimes an imaginary one, there seems to be room for an extra syllable: the pause absorbs it.

> *So wel they loved as olde bokes seye*   A 1064

The importance of this question—how far Chaucer went and how far the modern reader should go in resolving these ambiguities—is obvious. Once the trisyllabic foot is admitted among the other variations from a strict iambic pattern, the freer and richer becomes Chaucer's versification and the closer it comes to the practice of modern poets. For those who hold with the dogma of the strict decasyllable the question takes another form. It must be granted that when elision, contraction, and all the slurs are admitted nearly every line can be reduced to ten syllables—except of course those lines which have only nine (see below, p. 23). Since therefore their admission as a rule of Chaucer's practice *works*, it looks as though he allowed for them and hence they should be allowed. This is the pragmatic argument, for what it is worth.

One recalls now a dictum of Robert Bridges. Bridges, having laid it down at the outset that the typical line of *Paradise Lost* has ten syllables, and having made up rules to explain away the exceptions, felt obliged to yield ground in a NOTE:

We may say generally that Milton's system in *Par. Lost* was an attempt to keep blank verse decasyllabic by means of fictions: or . . . it may be said that he formulated the common conditions of those syllables which experience showed were oftenest and best used for trisyllabic places; and then worked within the line which he had thus drawn.[5]

Bridges makes another concession to reason: "though he printed *Th' Almighty*, etc., it cannot be supposed that he wished it to be so pronounced" (p. 50).

Now it will scarcely be supposed that Chaucer formulated any such system for himself: that has been left for the scholars. (Even Milton might have been a little surprised at Dr. Bridges' deductions.) To the rigorism of the Chaucerian specialists, Manly is a partial exception. "The tendency to reduce two syllables to

---

    This holy mayden that is so bright and shene   B 692
    Fro whennes cometh my wayling and my playnte   Tr. 1 408
Cf. O. Bischoff, "Über zweisilbige Senkung und epische Caesur bei Chaucer," *Engl. Studien* xxv (1898), 339-98, where more than 4000 lines are quoted or cited, and minutely classified to prove that Chaucer admitted no trisyllabic feet except at the so-called caesura.
    5. *Milton's Prosody*, Oxford, 1901. p. 19.

one in such cases as those discussed[6] and in many others seems to be based upon mechanical theories of versification inherited from the eighteenth century."

So much granted, it becomes a matter of drawing the line, and for that each reader must follow his own predilection, with such guidance as he can acquire from a sympathetic reading of the texts. Even if the poet himself had written *in thalighte* B 1660 (like Milton's "Th' Almighty"), one may assume, with Bridges, that he did not expect it to be so pronounced. The distinction is rarely made explicit, but it becomes real and important here: that scansion belongs to meter, the blueprint of verse, while prosody includes the departures from mechanical regularity and everywhere transcends scansion. The danger lies in confusing the two and in letting the one dictate to the other. The poets seldom make this mistake. However various are their habits of composition, the ear, the sound of the line, is their ultimate judge. But editors do often make the mistake: they like to emend according to *a priori* theory.

Hiatus, the opposite or avoidance of elision, seems also to be facultative with Chaucer rather than functional. Compare

For she koude of that art thė olde daunce	A 476
Wostow nat wel thė olde clerkes sawe	A 1163

with

And yet now thę olde Creon weylaway	A 938
Wel knowestow to wommen thę olde way	B 367
That wesshe the world fro the olde iniquitiee.	A 453

In

The othes that his couenantz assuren	A 1924
The open werre with woundes al bibled	A 2002
The okes olde and leyen hem on a rewe	A 2866

elision with *The* is optional—with hiatus, ten-syllable lines, without it, good nine-syllable lines. Compare

Yet hadde he but litel gold in cofre	A 298

6. The final *e* of *manciple* A 567, 586, the *Seuene* of B 4056 (which would have to pass as a monosyllable), the *statue of Mars* A 975, and the *many a* groups (*Canterbury Tales*, 1928, p. 128).

with hiatus *Yet haddė he,* but with elision *Yet haddę he* and due
emphasis on *Yet.* But how is one to know? The strong negative
ne is treated in two ways: without elision

Ne in noon other caas my leeue brother	A 1136
Of rasour ne of shere I wol thee yiue	A 2417
Of worthynesse ne of estaat ne age	A 2592
Ne may the venym voyden ne expelle,	A 2751

and with elison

Ne of Turnus with the hardy fiers corage	A 1945
Ne I ne axe noght tomorwe to haue victorie,	A 2239

and almost side by side

Ne in Belmarye ther nys so fel leoun	A 2630
Ne of his praye desireth so the blood.	A 2632

In

Withouten doute it may stonden so	A 1322

the pause may account for the hiatus, but not in

For thogh a wydwė hadde noght a sho.	A 253

One considerable objection to the decasyllabic theory is the
number of lines which plainly have only nine syllables.[7] Partly
out of deference to the theory and partly for convenience these
are called nine-syllable lines. The term headless is a bit gruesome,
acephalous is little better, and to call them lines with initial trun-
cation is cumbersome. They are too numerous to be waved aside
as textual errors: many of them could so easily have been avoided
by Chaucer by resort to his ready fillers. The Friar was familiar

7. Earlier scholars disputed the existence of such lines. For a thorough
defense of them, see Markus Freudenberger, *Über das Fehlen des Auftakts
in Chaucers heroischen Verse,* Erlangen diss., Leipzig, 1889, and in
Erlanger Beiträge, IV.—This term, nine-syllable line, may need further
definition, though it is commonly used and, I believe, commonly understood.
There are two objections to it, as to the term seven-syllable line for the short
couplet: (1) that it implies syllable-counting on Chaucer's part; and (2)
that when the normal line has a feminine ending there are actually eleven
syllables, and nine in the short couplet, so that the so-called nine-syllable
line may have actually ten syllables, and in the short couplet the seven-
syllable line may have actually eight syllables. This means simply that the
extra syllable of the feminine ending is not counted.

> *With frankeleyns ouer al in his contree*
> *And with worthy wommen of the toun.*   A 216 f.

And is made emphatic by the metrical stress, as much as to say:
Not only . . . but also. Hg and a few other manuscripts read
And eek. On this Manly (III, 423) comments: "S[keat]G[lobe]
R[obinson] adopt 'eek' from inadequate MS evidence to avoid a
nine-syllabled line, but textual evidence is overwhelmingly in
favor of Chaucer's frequent use of such lines in CT. In almost
every case a reader sensitive to rhythmic effects will find justification for these lines in the increased speed of movement." The
most familiar example is

> *Whan that Aprill with his shoures soote*   A 1

For a long time editors printed *Aprille*, thus adding the extra
syllable. But Manly (III, 421) has a long note which evidently
convinced Robinson and he now in his second edition reads
Aprill.[8]

These nine-syllable lines are of two sorts: those which like A
217 put a wanted stress on the first syllable:

> *Twenty bokes clad in blak or reed*   A 294
> *Yet hadde he but litel gold in cofre*   A 298
> *Who peynted the leoun tel me who,*   D 692

and, more often, those which appear to have no such justification:

> *For to deelen with no swich poraille*   A 247
> *In a gowne of faldyng to the knee*   A 391
> *For to stonden at my iuggement.*   A 788

A few others may be classed as ambiguous in this respect, e.g.,

> *Sholden spille a quarter of a tere.*   *Tr.* v 880

Different again are

> *Yong, fressh, strong, and hardy as lyoun;*
> *Trewe as steel in ech condicioun.*   *Tr.* v 830 f.

8. Robinson was not convinced elsewhere, for he still retains *eek* in A
217. Manly sought in vain for examples of *Aprille*. In *Tr.* I, 156 and III, 360,
however, the word has three syllables, *Aperil*, and could be so read in A 1,
with inversion of the first three feet. But who would care to do so?

Quite unusual, with its spondees in the first and fifth place, is

> *Ech man for hymself ther is noon oother.*   A 1182

Sometimes the line is wholly trochaic:

> *Now it shyneth now it reyneth faste*   A 1535
> *Graunted on the morwe, at his requeste.*   *Tr.* v 949

A few lines, here and there, are not so easily classed. For instance,

> *Eek Plato seith who so kan hym rede*   A 741

The editors, following Ha⁴ alone (a weak reed) insert *that* after *so.* Alternatively, one could take *seith* as two syllables. But as Manly notes (III, 425), "sometimes, as here [Chaucer seems to have] omitted the unstressed syllable after the caesural pause." Such lines have been called broken-backed or Lydgate lines, because Lydgate seems to have favored them.[9] Often a 'dramatic' pause takes the place of the missing syllable, as in

> *As seyde hym self moore than a curat*   A 219
> *Qui la quod he Peter it am I*   B 1404
> *But euere folwed my appetit*   D 623
> *Thow art myn wyf noon oother I haue*   E 1063
> *Of that he spak no man heren myghte*   *Tr.* II 1120
> *He song, as who seyth, "somewhat I brynge,"*   II 1309

Sometimes a conjunction seems to have fallen out, thus spoiling a balance, as in

> *Beautee and youthe baudrye richesse*
> *Charmes and force lesynges flaterye*   A 1925 f.
> *Al were he short long blak or whit*   D 624
> *I mene of Mark Mathew Luc and Iohn*   B 2141
> *After the text of Crist Poul and Iohn*   D 1647
> *Wisdom, Estaat, Drede, and Governaunce*   Pite 41
> *That hot, cold, hevy, lyght, moyst, and dreye.*   PF 380

A few examples may be more apparent than real, owing to faulty text, as

9. Cf. E. P. Hammond, *English Verse between Chaucer and Surrey,* Durham, N. C., 1927, pp. 84-85.

> *Was complet and passed were also*   B 4379
> *My tale is doon for my wit is thynne*   E 1682
> *When Diomede on hors gan hym dresse.*   Tr. v 37

Most of the above lines have been 'improved' by scribes or editors
to conform to the conventional pattern, but one at least is too good
as it stands to warrant emendation:

> *Sholde this child softe wynde and wrappe.*   E 583

As Miss Hammond puts it (*Manual*, p. 486),

> *Or breke it at a rennyng with his hed*   A 551

has as much right to be called a five-stress line as

> *But thow wis, thow woost, thow maist, thou art al.*   Tr. i 1052

One can go even farther and say that

> *Bare ruined choirs where late the sweet birds sang*
> *Other sins only speak; murder shrieks out*
> *Charmed magic casements opening on the foam*

are in the same meter as

> *Of hand, of foot, of lip, of eye, of brow*
> *The curfew tolls the knell of parting day*
> *So all day long the noise of battle rolled,*

however different their rhythm is.

We call these lines iambic because their prevailing metrical
pattern is a series of iambs; but in Chaucer's language there is,
owing to the syllabic endings, a large proportion of words which
are natural trochees: *shoures soote, tendre croppes, yonge sonne,
smale foweles, straunge strondes, ferne halwes, sondry londes,
shires ende, hooly blisful martir*, and so on. This, together with
the feminine rimes, often produces the effect of trochaic rhythm
and makes a kind of counterpoint to the iambic metrical scheme:
*The droght of March, Of which vertu, Inspired hath, That slepen
al the nyght, So priketh hem nature*, and so on. There are not
only scattered lines which are wholly trochaic, but a number also
of nine-syllable lines with feminine endings which move to the
same trochaic tune:

Whan that Aprill with his shoures soote   A 1
Sholden spille a quarter of a tere.   *Tr.* v 880

The older books made a good deal of this difference between rising and falling rhythm, but in practice the two work together easily and the distinction is mainly technical.

3. THE SHORT COUPLET

AFTER his early translation of RR Chaucer employed the short couplet only twice: in BD, also early, and in HF, of uncertain date, usually said to be *ca.* 1380. For his Romaunt of the Rose he naturally followed the meter of the original, but about his handling of it one hesitates to speak definitely, for we have only one manuscript and Thynne's edition of 1532, both unsatisfactory as to text. In Fragment A the lines, apart from editorial emendation, are fairly regular iambic octosyllables with a sprinkling of seven-syllable lines. They are rather smoother than in BD.

Skeat dismissed the short couplet as merely a shortened form of the five-stress line, but this will not do at all. The movement is bound to be different. Robinson (2nd ed., p. 898) puts the case obliquely: "The authorities agree in supporting many readings which are either unsatisfactory in sense or metrically inferior to most of Chaucer's verse." One asks: by what standard metrically inferior? By lacking a syllable here and there, Chaucer may allude to the headless or seven-syllable lines, but it is more likely that he means to say that the meter is a little rough and irregular— which it is. But rough and irregular compared to what?

For this couplet Chaucer would have had two models: the octosyllabics of French poetry and the native English tradition, as in *Owl and Nightingale*, many of the romances, homiletic poems like the *Prick of Conscience*, or the short line of the stanzaic *Pearl*, all of which were accentual, not syllabic. Chaucer's modification of this is obvious when one sets side by side his Sir Thopas and the *Sir Gy* which he was making fun of. Let one example suffice:

> *And in his hand a launcegay*   B 1942
> *In his hand a gode swerd he bar.*[1]

In a word, the meter of BD and HF is midway between the syllabism of the French octosyllabic and the freedom (or incompetence) of the minstrels' work. It is accentual, yet restricted by such canons of correctness and smoothness as he preferred when writing the five-stress line (which is not *lewed*). One might call it a compromise if the word did not have disagreeable associations.

The couplets of BD are four-stress iambic, with the usual elisions and contractions and no more than the usual forced or misplaced stresses,—as in

> *I have gret wonder, be this lyght*   1
> *I was war of a man in blak;*   445

or the opposite, a strong syllable in the weak position:

> *And this quene highte Alcyone*   65
> *Right thus this king Seys loste his lyf.*   75

Often what at first seems irregular is due to an unexpected inversion:

> *While men loved the lawe of kinde*   56
> *She longed so after the king*   83
> *Ne she koude no reed but oon.*   105

There is perhaps more than the usual uncertainty in pronouncing syllabic *e*, for in this meter the anapest is more likely than in the longer line and it is less necessary to invoke elision:

> *To doo hir erande, and he com ner*   134
> *And shewe hir shortly, hit ys no nay*   147
> *That had affrayed me out of my slep*   296
> *For nother to cold nor hoot yt was*   342
> *My wyt is foly, my day ys nyght,*   610

1. Laura Hibbard Loomis, "Chaucer and the Auchinlech MS," *Essays and Studies in Honor of Carleton Brown*, New York, 1940, pp. 111-28; p. 122. For more of the same, a half-hour's reading of fourteenth-century short couplets will do. *Sir Orfeo* would be a fair test; or *Pearl*, which is neither *lyght* nor *lewed*,—though its use of alliteration makes it very different from Chaucer in tone.

and so on to the end of the poem,

> *My lady, that is so fair and bryght.*   1180

Elision, syncope, etc. may be possible for the syllabic rigorists, in such lines as

> *Was wery, and thus the dede slep*   127
> *Me thoghte wonder yf hit were so*   233
> *All was forgeten, and that was sene.*   413

The word *sor(o)we* must be reckoned with. In

> *Joye or sorowe, wherso hyt be*   10

it is disyllabic, and in

> *For sorwe ful nygh wood she was,*   104

and also in line 100 where it stands at the end of the line. But compare

> *Such sorowe this lady to her tok*   95
> *For in your sorwe there lyth no red,*   203

where it must be a monosyllable—if the anapest is to be avoided—and in

> *For sorwful ymagynacioun*   14

probably monosyllabic, *sorw-*. (Skeat substituted *sory* to make elision look easier.)

Lines of this sort offer no great difficulty, and their mild liberties clear the way for the goodly number which without such warning seem really irregular and which have left a bad impression. Properly considered they illustrate the latitude which Chaucer permitted himself in this meter. Take a few examples.

> *With good wille, body, herte and al*   116, 768
> *Blew, bryght, clere was the ayr*   340
> *Men, hors, houndes, and other thyng*   349
> *For hit was, on to beholde*   405
> *The wondres me mette in my sweven*   442
> *I was able to have lerned tho*   786
> *Hit happed that I cam on a day*   805
> *Symple, of good mochel, noght to wyde*   861

Was whit, rody, fressh, and lyvely hewed 905
And I hooly hires and everydel 1041
That was the ten woundes of Egipte. 1207

But these and their like melt into the metrical background and enrich the texture. Two lines, at least, show a bold irregularity which one hopes was deliberate:

With a gret horn blew thre mot 376
As for her was al harm hyd. 932

(The editors have of course improved these away.)

As there are lines which seem too long and which may without emendation be read with trisyllabic feet (the rigorists permitting), so there are shorter, seven-syllable, lines (on the same principle as the nine-syllable five-stress lines):

To noon erthly creature 19
And this quene highte Alcyone 65
Slepe, or I had red this tale 228
What harm was; or elles she. 997

A few lines which might be seven-syllabled are remedied by invoking hiatus:

I ferde worse al the morwe 99
That made hir to slepe sone 130
I wil yive hym the alderbeste 246
With his tayle he wol stynge 640
Of Troye and of Ilyoun. 1248

There are other lines which are reduced to order by elision:

Me thoghte wonder yf hit were so 233
All was forgeten, and that was sene 413
But hyt may never the rather be doo; 562

and others which seem to have real anapests:

That had affrayed me out of my slep 296
That thogh Argus, the noble countour 435
My wit ys foly, my day is nyght 610
I shal ryght blythely, so God me save 755
For-why I tok hyt of so yong age. 793

In sum, the numerous lines—and they are not so numerous as to destroy the pattern—which seem irregular may be explained in one or two ways. Either we hold that Chaucer never wrote an irregular line, especially in his early work, and amend the text accordingly; or we recognize that in the short couplet he admitted greater freedom than in the longer heroic line, because he followed a different principle, a system influenced by the native accentual meters.

The meter of HF differs from that of BD in being more uniform and smooth. There is however a larger proportion of seven-syllable lines—sometimes emphasizing the first word or syllable—

> *Causen hem avisiouns,*   40

but more often not. They may occur in clusters or there may be a stretch of thirty-five to forty lines without one.[2]

Hiatus, as vouched for by the scansion, occurs in *The armes* 144, *shulde his* 237, *Epistle of* 379, *moste have* 410, *place every* 733, *substaunce ys* 768, *speche and* 1028, *nyste how* 1049, *faire on* 1050 (Robinson reads *fair*, which gives an inferior line), *stone of* 1184 (Robinson reads *ston*, but the *-e* is possibly an old dative and *stone* makes a better verse), *the olde* 1433, *ordre of* 1905, *unnethe in* 2041.

The plainest example of anapest is in

> *Of estats, and eke of regiouns,*   1970

though of course one could read *stats*.

The spondaic cadence is frequent—

> *And ther he shulde his folk fynde*   237

and in a dozen more. To be noted is *fayreste* 281.

There are fewer examples of wrenched accent than in BD: *falslý* 389, *foréstes* 899, *wyndówes* 1191, *pilgrímes* (*:tymes*) 2122, only here in rime.

2. Cf. Edgar F. Shannon, "Chaucer's Use of the Octosyllabic Verse in the Book of the Duchess and in the House of Fame," *JEGP* XII (1913), 277-94. Shannon counted 136 seven-syllable lines in BD (10.2 per cent) against 294 in HF (13.6 per cent). Inversion of the first foot is more frequent in BD than in HF; on the other hand, inversion of the third foot is more frequent in HF than in BD.

A few lines are made of strict iambs:

> *Hyr lyf, hir love, hir lust, hir lord*   258
> *Or voys, or noyse, or word, or soun,*   819

and one of all trochees,

> *Snowes, hayles, reynes, wyndes;*   967

but along with these are, for variety,

> *Bridd, fissh, best, or him or here*   1003
> *Blak, bloo, grenyssh, swartish red.*   1647

Some few lines are troublesome. A weak stress in the first foot, so common in the longer line, is more disturbing in the shorter:

> *Of her loves, or in what place*   86
> *Of Decembre the tenthe day*   111
> *Of the goddys celestials;*   460

and unexpected inversions have to be watched:

> *How that yet she shulde here al this*   705
> *Myghte ther all the armes seen*   1337
> *But these be no suche tydynges*   1894
> *With the nones that thou wolt do so.*   2099

There is certainly an anapest, warranted by the internal rime, in

> *And right so breketh it when men speketh,*   780

and others probably, as in

> *That ther come entryng into the halle.*   1527

There are two lines which Swinburne might have written:

> *Me, fleynge, in a swap he hente*   543
> *Me caryinge in his clawes starke.*   545

Yet these peculiarities (they are more evident in Book iii, where Chaucer was hurrying) can be managed, and in a poem of over two thousand lines they do not stand out conspicuously. Although there are no sufficient grounds for dating HF, as there are indeed no agreed conclusions about its meaning or intention,

the consensus to place it near 1380 would suggest ٧
supports, a definite interval between it and BD, ٠
which Chaucer was acquiring facility, even some ٠
facility" which Byron felt about this meter. The H.
finished and Chaucer never used its meter again.

4. RIMES

And eke to me it ys a gret penaunce,
Syth rym in Englissh hath such skarsete.
—Compleynt of Venus

UNLESS one holds, against the prevailing view, that Chaucer
did not pronounce the syllabic *-e* at the end of a line, two
things are obvious. One is that we find a much larger proportion
of feminine rimes than in modern English verse; the other is
that they introduce an anapestic movement from line to line
which is commonly denied within the line. Thus *his shoures soote
The droghte of March* must be heard as ∪/∪|/∪∪/∪/. In the first
hundred lines of the General Prologue thirty have masculine
rimes (including lines which end on a secondary accent) and
seventy feminine; in the next hundred the proportion is 46 to
54, in the next 50 to 50. In stanzaic poems the proportions are
somewhat different. For example in ClT the feminine rimes in
the first hundred outnumber the masculine by 76 to 24, in the
second hundred by 74 to 26, in the third by 70 to 30. Similarly
in MLT they are 63 to 37, 67 to 33, 76 to 24. Skeat noted a stretch
of four stanzas in the *Troilus* (III 407-34) with no masculine
rimes. No one has made an exhaustive computation, but it is
clear that feminine predominate over masculine rimes.

These feminine rimes take several forms. They may be (1)
quasi-trisyllabic as *victorie glorie* A 2405/06, *maryed taryed* B
3461/63, *scatered yflatered* D 1969/70, *seuene heuene* D 2005/06,
narowe arowe Anel 183/85; *delyvered toshyvered* PF 491/93; or
(2) broken (Schipper's term), i.e., made up of two words, as
houndes yfounde ys BD 377/78, *beryis merye is* B 4155/56, *sweu-
enys sweuene is* B 4111/12, *Rome to me* A 671/72, *woundid wounde
hid* B 102/03, *agon is onys* D 9/10, *youthe allowthe* F 675/76,

werkis derk is G 64/66, *Tyme by me* G 1204/05, *harmed harm hyd* BD 931/32, *Chek her! chekker* BD 659/60. Exceptional is *lyte is dytees* HF 620/21 because the full form should be *ditee is* and the rime therefore involves syncope rather than elision.

Whether masculine or feminine the rime may double back to include the preceding foot, as *desperacioun dampnacioun* ABC 21/23, *conclusioun illusioun* F 1263/64, *affecciouns protecciouns* F 55/56, *nyghtertale nyghtyngale* A 97/98. In the Parson's Prologue there is an interesting series: *meditacioun correccioun* I 55/56 followed by *protestacioun correccioun* I 59/60—a double rime in *-acioun* though in neighboring couplets—and then the Host repeats the Parson's word, with courteous patience, *meditacioun* I 71 but with a different riming word (*adoun*).

A great many rimes take advantage of secondary accent. Miss Hammond calls them "cheap," and so they are when they rely on common suffixes like *-ly*, *-les*, *-aunce*, etc. Chaucer is rather free with them. Cf. *Tr.* II 1717/19/20 where all three b-rimes are *-ly* and *Tr.* I 779/81/82, PF 590/92/93 where the b-rimes are in *-les*. But there are others, like *corages pilgrimages* A 11/12, which escape this charge.

A very special variety of rime, which may be called spondaic rime, occurs very early in Chaucer's work and continues throughout, namely, rimes with words ending in *-(n)esse and -yng(e)*, when the meaning comes from the preceding syllable but the metrical stress falls on the ending. These may be approached from two directions: acoustically by way of lines which end with a natural spondaic foot—

This bok ne spak but of such things	BD 57
Had such pittee and such rowthe	97
To doo hir erande, and he com ner	134
Now understond wel, and tak kep;	138

and secondly by way of words in which the ending has a regular secondary accent. A single couplet in BD illustrates both aspects:

Defaute of slep and hevynesse	
Hath sleyn my spirit of quyknesse.	25-26

Some of the earliest examples are ambiguous partly because of the possible influence of French accentuation: *distresse humblesse maistresse goodnesse* ABC 106/08/09/11 and *goodnesse maistresse governouresse witnesse* ABC 138/40/41/43. There is no example in Pite. BD has many: *quyknesse* 26, *siknesse* 36, and so in 109/10, 607, 701/02, 797, 828, 993, 1040, 1060. Those in *-yng* begin with *slepying* 230, *huntyng* 350, and continue to the end: 599/600, 611/12, 633/34, 801, 870, 959/60, 995/96, 1313, 1328. In HF there are more than a dozen rimes in *-esse*, and those in *-ynge* are numerous: in Book I only two; in the 582 lines of Book II, seven; and in the 1168 lines of Book III nineteen; or one in every 63 lines of the last two Books. (This is partly due to the repetition of the word *tydynges*.) In MancT, presumably early, there are *witnesse* H 284, *goodnesse* 322, *werkyng* 210. In the late Truth, *goodnesse* 24.

This kind of rime seems to occur only in Middle English and may have come to Chaucer, and Gower, from such rimes as *chantant tant* in *Roman de la Rose*—which are distinctly different in French however, because the 'accent" in French words is different. It looks sometimes like an easy shift and so subject to abuse, like the suffix rimes in *-ly,* etc.; but when heard with an attentive ear it has a very peculiar and striking effect. It directs attention from the riming syllable to the preceding root syllable; it slows the pace as with a kind of *tempo rubato*; and for the moment almost completely alters the rhythm. Take

So fer am I from his help in derknesse   *Tr.* I 18

The preceding rime *unliklynesse* prepares the ear for an *-esse,* either with full stress or as a secondary accent. Then comes *derknesse,* which is a surprise because it goes /\ u instead of the expected u / u. Now the *in,* which should theoretically bear the metrical stress, is reduced to u. The result is therefore neither / u / u nor u / / u nor yet u /\ u, but something like ù /\ u, which is contrary to all the rules. It is much the same with *an hierdesse Tr.* I 653. The effect is still different when instead of *in* or *an* (neither quite stressed nor quite unstressed) one meets *may don gladnesse Tr.* I 19, for *don* merits the expected stress while *in* does

not. Parallel examples of the other ending are in *wynnynge* 1 199
and *of youre lyvynge* 1 197.

All this is further complicated by an apparent inconsistency
or accepted variation in the use of these words within the line.
Compare

> And caughte ayeyn his firste pléyinge chere　　　1 280
>
> Gan for to like hire mévynge and hire chere　　　1 289

with

> And whil she was dwellýnge in that cite.　　　　1 129

Then there are intermediate forms as in *whistlynge* A 2337 (for
which Robinson prints *whistelynge*).

Somewhat analogous are the rimes which require a shift of
the normal accent. Chaucer enjoyed in fact a certain latitude in
the accentuation of many words. Proper names were likely to
vary; words of French origin are often accented either way (e.g.,
pite, pitous, nature, vertu, servaunt, etc.); so also prepositions and
adverbs like *unto, therof*; also *whilom*; and so on. Certain other
words could be accented either way: *félawe* A 648, *feláwe* A 650;
manhóod A 756, *mánhood Tr.* ii 676. Many words which are normally trochaic become iambic in rime: *míllere* A545 but *Millére*
A 542 in rime; *dággere* A 392 but *daggére* A 113 in rime; so likewise *window* A 1075, A 3676; *forheed* A 3310, A 154; *answere*
D 910, E 2266; *chaffare* B 138, 139; *miteyn* C 372, 373; *Thomas* D
1832 in the same line. Cf. *Bigýnnyng* F 717, but *bígynnyng* A 3007
in rime.

In BD Chaucer allowed himself even greater latitude: *Trewely*
whether in rime or not is usually trisyllabic, though here and there
it may be contracted to a disyllable, but in BD 687 it seems clearly
to be *trewlý*. In BD 1151 and only there *ladý* (and cf. *Tr.* v 1516
where *lady* within the line seems to be accented on the second
syllable); so also *goodlý* BD 1283, *frendlý* BD 852, *hoolý* BD 688,
746, 1269. *Worthi* occurs once in rime PF 635, and *unworthý* E
359. In *Tr.* 1 988 *redý*.

Among other examples note *archér* H 108; also in Sir Thopas
B 1929.

A step further leads to the employment of unemphatic words

in rime, especially in enjambement. For example in the *Troilus*:
ther was / Dwellynge a lord i 64-65; *that he / Knew wel* i 67-68;
she / Was ii 604-05; *heede to / That* iv 852-53; and most striking
help me from / The deth i 535-36; and with a whole line intervening

> *for I have*
> *As ferforthlich as I have had ƙonnynge,*
> *Ben youres al.*[1]   *Tr.* iii 100-2

Echo rime (Fr. *rime riche*) is fairly common in Chaucer.
The words are the same but different in meaning, though the
difference may be slight. It occurs first, chronologically, in ABC
26/31 *heere* (here) *heere* (hear), and in BD 883/84 *herte* (hurt)
herte (heart). The most familiar example is A 17/18 *seke* (seek)
seeke (sick), where both vowels are $\bar{e}^1$. Often the echo is varied
with a difference in the vowel, as *se* (see) *see* (ocean) A 1955/56,
3031/32, the first having $\bar{e}^1$, the second $\bar{e}^2$. Examples in KtT are:
may May A 1461/62, *lief leef* A 1837/38, *armes armes* A 2247/48,
queynte queynte A 2333/34, *cas caas* A 2357/58, *fare* (infin.)
fare (p.ple), A 2435/36, *highte highte* A 2919/20. Other examples
are noted passim, e.g., *style style* F 105/06, *fern fern* F 255/56.
There are several examples of identical rime, i.e., where there is
no real difference in the meaning of the words. Examples in *CT*
are: one in Thopas (*contree*, B 1908/12); two in ClT (*smale*, E
380/83; *in reste in pees and reste*, E 1129/32); four in MkT
(*sente*, B 3400/03; *two*, B3640/43; *broghte*, B 3882/84; *he*, B

---

1. One recalls Keats's "ofttimes hath / Charmed magic casements."
Chaucer could have seen something like this in Froissart. Cf.

> *Et les chavaus à mener, ƙar*
> *Esprouver volt* (i, 271),

"sans nul si / Gai" (ii, 134-35), "pour ycès / Four-faitures" (ii, 154), "et
pour / Toutes ses oevres" (ii, 203), "Imagination, a ces / Mos" (ii, 243);
and such enjambement as "lors / Que" (i, 2), "si / Que" (i, 309), "affin /
Que" (iii, 13), "*en fin* / De" (iii, 60). The references are to ed. Scheler,
Bruxelles, 1870-72. There are many other resemblances: sentences running
through several lines, the frequency of echo rime, the repetition of rime
pairs, and such double rimes as "en cor : encor" (*La Prison amoureuse*,
49-50, 1306-7), "raison : s'aise on" (*ibid.* 3315/16)—though in Chaucer
these rimes hardly went beyond words in *-acioun*. He never went so far as
rimes like "souffisance : souffisant. Ce," "presente : present te," "souv-
eraine : souverain ne" (*La Cour de May*, 243/44, 569/70, 611/12).

3904/07). All these occur in stanzas. There are two line cases: in MLT *woot,* B 436/39, and *wey* in MillProl, A 3133/34. In the *Troilus* there are two clear examples: *to and fro,* II 513/16, and *was,* V 975/78; and two which are debateable, *heed* (part of the body and part of a bed), III 964/57, and *moore,* V 1353/56.

What may be regarded as a sub-form of echo rime are such combinations as *serued reserued* A 187/88 (cf. A 1231/32, 2379/80), *oon noon* A 317/18, 679/80, *nas was* A 321/22, *stonde understonde* A 745/46, *also so* A 811/12, *recorde acorde* A 829/30, PF 608/09, *come ouercome* A 2799/00, *obserue deserue* B 1821/22, *alighte lighte* B 1660/61; and also such broken rimes as *clerkis clerk is* B 4425/26, *placis place is* D 1767/68; and many more.

There is at least one triple echo rime: *ladishippe shipe* (reward) *shippe* Anel 191/94/95.

Now and then Chaucer turns to a dialect for rime—to the North for *telles elles* BD 73/74, *falles halles* BD 257/58, *tydynges brynges* HF 1907/08. Kentish rimes are more common, e.g., *brest lest* (for *lust*) A 2983/84, E 617/19, *keste* F 350, *Tr.* III 1129 (but *kiste* III 1252), *kesse* E 1057. Sometimes he turns in unexpected directions: *entewnes Tewnes* BD 309/10 (as though in 1958 one should rime vicuña: Tristan da Cunha); or to *Spayne* HF 1117 for a place with high mountains.

Scattered throughout are a number of imperfect or approximate rimes to which Chaucer seems to have had recourse when none better occurred to him. Such for instance are *sauith significauit* A 661/62 and *Dauit eructauit* D 1933/34. In C 291/92 he rimes *aduocatz* (spelled *aduocas* by several scribes) with *allas.* In Scogan 15/17 he rimes *goddes* with *forbode is; goddes* is ambiguous; if it refers to the *goddis sevene* 3 the rime is normal, but if it refers to *Venus* II, as the context implies, it is a clipped form of *goddesse.*

In a few places what look like irregular rimes have been removed by the editors, as in BD 79/80 *terme yerne* (where *erme* is doubtless correct). In *Tr.* II 884 *sike* seems to rime with *endite white,* but *syte* (grieve) is possible. In *Tr.* II 933/35/36 the rimes are *riden abiden yeden.* The last word clearly means 'went' (cf. *dede yede* G 1140/41 and *nede yede* G 1280/81, with *ē¹*). This is called by Skeat (VI, xlix) "one of the most licentious rimes," comparing the doublets *yeve yive*, but the vowel of these is short.

In WBT Chaucer rimes *elenge* : *chalenge* (D 1199/1200). *Elenge* is derived from æ-leng(e), both noun and adjective. The development from ŋ to ndʒ is similar to the more familiar nc to ntʃ (benche < benc, þenchen < þencan, etc.). Cf. Wright, *Elementary M.E. Grammar*, §§ 262; 294. It occurs in only a few words, with raising of *e* to *i*: cringe < crengan, singe < sengan, springe < sprengan, swinge < swengan, twinge < twengan; and hinge < ME heng. NED says, s.v. *hinge*, that the palatalization of *g* is not clearly evidenced before 1590. Chaucer's rime, however, though an isolated example, would put the change much earlier. Chaucer permitted himself two approximate rimes in *aventure honoure,* Venus 22/23; and *Chaunte-pleure -ure,* Anel 320/24/25/26/27/29/30/31.

For convenience Chaucer has a few doublets, e.g., *ek eke, her here, ther there,*—in all of which the *-e* is unhistorical, but the *-e* forms can be used in rime. Also the emphatic form of *wel,* as in *wel deel.* Also the reduced form of the pronouns *me* and *the,* as in *Rome to me, youthe allowthe.*

In some places an originally short vowel appears to rime with a long vowel: *spade hade* A 553/54, *hade blade* A 617/18; but the spelling *hade* probably indicates that the vowel had been lengthened in the open syllable. This is not true, however, of *was caas* A843/44, *set fet* BD 501/02, *vp on goon* G 562/63. Cf. also the foreign words: *Aurelius amorus* F 1499/1500, *Apius lecherus* C 265/66, *noblesse Boece* D 1167/68, HF 971/72, *-nesse Lucresse* Anel 81/82. Sometimes there is apparent inconsistency due to the rule that long vowels were shortened in closed syllables but retained their length in inflected forms: *brĕst* but *brḗstes* (Wright, *Elementary Middle English Grammar* §97) etc.; then the vowel might pass indifferently as either long or short; as in *bĕst* (adv.) *brĕst* BD 173/74, *fḗstes bḗstes* BD 433/34 (*but also ēst beest* F 459/60) and *forĕst bḗst* (beast) LGW 842/43, *tempĕst ḗst* B 491/93; but *forĕstes bḗstes* HF 899/900, *bḗstes tempĕstes* HF 965/66, 1967/68. There is also some uncertainty about the superlative adverb, whether *bĕst* or *bēste.* In *Tr.* v 1429 ff. the a-rimes are *festes bi-*

hestes and the b-rimes are *best* (adv.) *west lest*—with the further complication that in *if that the lest* the verb should be subjunctive, *leste*. Cf. *Tr.* ii 1051 *If the lest* (:*west*) and *Tr.* ii 1394 *best* (for *beste*). Obviously Chaucer gave himself latitude in such details.

In F 961/62 *neighebour honour* and HF 649/50 *neyghebores dores* the rimes have been questioned, but both are correct.

Quite remarkable are the rimes in the *Go, litel book* stanza, *Tr.* v 1786-90: the a-rimes are *tragedye comedye* and the b-rimes *dye nenvie poesie*.

Two unusual rimes in Thopas are doubtless due to the parody element. *Tespye Fairye* B 1989/92 and *Fairye symphonye* 2004/5 are normal; but *chiualry drury* (without -*e*) B 2084/85 and *chiualry* 2092 are not Chaucer's usual forms. The rimes *Thopas solas* B 1904/07 are normal, but *Thopas gras* (grace) 2020/21 are not, for Chaucer's regular form is *grace*. (Cf. *place grace* B 1910/13). Again, *was gras* (grass) B 1968/9 is correct, but in the same stanza *plas solas* is a 'minstrel' rime, for Chaucer's regular forms are *solas* (n.) and *place*. (Cf. *grace solace* HF 2007/08, where *solace* is infin.) The situation here is complicated by the fact that *was gras solas* are good rimes, and the rime scheme of the stanza is ambiguously *aabaab* or *aabccb*. It is possible that in the stanza B 2081-86 the a-rimes *charitee free* are meant, in anticipation of the later change in pronunciation, to match *chiualry drury* and the scheme would then be *aabaab* rather than *aabccb*. For this fifteenth-century pronunciation compare the next to last stanza of Compleynt to his Lady. The text there is bad and the editors have emended as seemed best to them. But the last four lines of each stanza rime *cddc*, and in this stanza the manuscripts have *verrayly be* for the c-rimes. *Verrayly* is suspect because it repeats the stanza's a-rimes. Yet there has to be a first time.

A considerable complication arises from the rimes in open (slack) and close (tense) *e* and *o*. (Open *ē* is represented as $\bar{e}$ or $\bar{e}^2$; close *ē* as *ẹ* or $\bar{e}^1$; similarly $\bar{\rho}$, $\bar{o}^2$, *ọ*, $\bar{o}^1$). For the most part Chaucer observes these distinctions in his rimes, but there are a few words which he allows to rime with either quality indifferently, i.e., open *e* and close *e*, open *o* and close *o* together. Skeat has a convenient list of these in Oxford Chaucer vi, xlv-xlvii, and a shorter one in his *Rime-Index to the Troilus*, following a lengthy discussion.

The following words may rime either way: *eche* (to eke), *leche, speche*; *dede* (dead), *drede* (n. and vb.), *hede* (heed), *rede* (advise). In the suffix *-hede* the *e* is nearly always open. Again, *sene, ysene* (adj.), *shene; slepe; bere* (bier) *dere* (dear) *fere* (fear), *here* (hear) *lere* (teach) *yere* (year). *Bihete, forlete, mete* (dream), *shete, strete. Eve, leve, bileve, leve* (permit); *done. Hore, lore, more, sore, yore* all have $\bar{o}^2$, but sometimes rime with words which have $\bar{o}^1$. The frequent rimes in *-ee* have regularly $\bar{e}^1$, except *see* (sea) which is properly $\bar{e}^2$.

In many of these words the quality of the vowel was affected by dialectal and other influences. Cf. p. 38 above. Chaucer's employment of them in rime is both natural and reasonable, and it may well be that in his own speech some of the distinctions were not clearly marked. In sum, it is not a question of vindicating Chaucer's accuracy in riming (as Skeat was concerned to do in answer to Lounsbury) so much as illustrating both his latitude on the side of convenience and his artistic results in choosing and rejecting. The main point is that a reader should accustom himself to observe closely how Chaucer fits his rimes.[2]

2. For an exhaustive treatment of one part of the evidence see Victor Langhans, "Der Reimvokal *e* bei Chaucer," *Anglia* XLV (1921), 221-82 (short *e*) and 297-392 (long *e*). This is partly a rebuttal of the article in *Anglia* I, by ten Brink, who would solve the problems solely by reference to the A. S. original of each word. The extensive lists and tables of Langhans are not easy to follow, but the upshot is—not unexpectedly—that in rime Chaucer almost always observes the quantity of *e*, and the quality regularly; but sometimes for convenience or necessity, or because his London English showed a mixture of dialects, he would rime together words with e^1 and e^2. For example, *neede* is used twenty-nine times as e^1, but nineteen times with the handy words *drede, dede* it rimes with e^2; *dede* was e^2 in Chaucer's dialect but rimes twelve times as e^1 against seventy-six as e^2; *drede* the same, the proportions being 105 e^2 and thirty-seven for e^1. He had available only four words with final -e^2 (*sle, stre, se, ye*), therefore he resorted to *he, me, we, thee*, all e^1. *Clene, mene, lene* have e^2 but often rime with e^1, e.g., *clene. seene* A 134, *lene yseene* A 592. *There* rimes fifty times with e^2, only twice with e^1; *were* fifty-six times with e^2, only five times with e^1; *yere* divides about evenly between e^1 and e^2. That Chaucer well recognized the distinction is evidenced by a passage in Anelida's compleynt (see p. 100) and by the Triple Roundel of Merciles Beaute (see p. 94); when he dis-

There are no statistics and no formulated standards on how often the same pair of rimes may be happily repeated. A few notes on the General Prologue and the Knight's Tale will serve first to illustrate Chaucer's habits. For PF and *Troilus* see below pp. 105, 43 f.

Everyone recognizes the propriety of echoing *corages pilgrymages* A 11/12 by *pilgrimage corage* A 21/22, contrasting the general and particular, with a playful contrast also between the *corages* of the little birds and the devoutness of the narrator. But what should be said of the six pairs in *-ye* in the first eighty-six lines, repeated five times later in the General Prologue, the last two as close together as 413/14 and 419/20? Or the cheap rimes in *-ly* 105/06 and 123/24? Or *-ly* 761/62 and followed by *-ye* 763/64? Or *degree be* 55/56 and *See he* 59/60? Or *breed deed* 147/48 (just after *bledde fedde*) and *reed forheed* 153/54? Or *confessioun* 218, 221 (with different rime words)? Or *heed reed* 293/94 and *heede neede* 303/04? Or *ytaught naught* 755/56 and *bythoght noght* eleven lines below? Or *weye pleye* 771/72, *seye weye* 779/80, *weye tweye* 791/92, *withseye weye* 805/6? Or *so mo* 807/08, 849/50 and *also so* 811/12? Then there are the series in *-er, -ere* 111/14; *-eres, -ere,* 231/34; *-oun, oon* 315-19. These things go as they go. Sometimes they are a matter of chance (if that word is ever justifiable in artistic work) or of convenience or necessity, and sometimes they depend on the subject in hand. Sometimes they show careful artistry whether we see it or not.

The situation in KtT is different because that is a long poem with recurrent motifs and something now and then that savors of epic repetition. For example, *brother* and *oother* rime together four times; *I* and the handy *-ly* six times; and so with *colde olde*, *lyf wyf*, and so on. The sequence *take stake, take make,* and fourfold *ytake stake* in A 2551/52, 2555/56, 2617/18, 2641/42, 2647/48, 2723/24 are due to the tournament; but there is no such apparent reason for *weye seye* 1121/22, *pley fey, pleye tweye* A 1125/28; or the *-esse* rimes A 1249/50, 1255/56; or *heed deed* 1707/08 repeated 1725/26; or *oon anoon* 1771/72 and ten lines later *oon agoon*

regarded it he must have done so consciously, except of course when in his own language the quality was ambivalent.

(repeated 1813/14); or *cheere heere, were beere* 2897/00. The *-ye* rimes, prominent in GenlProl, start in KtT at the seventh line (865) and recur in some twenty pairs (frequently with *Emelye*) before the famous line

> *Allone withouten any compaignye,*   A 2779

and thereafter eleven times, almost like a refrain, to the final couplet with *Emelye compaignye* 3107/08.

There is next the matter of repeating the same rime sounds in adjacent lines or stanzas, and also the use over and over of the same words in rime.

A look at the rimes in Book 1 of the *Troilus* will serve as a clue to those of the other Books. The citations are now for convenience by stanzas rather than lines and the Books indicated by arabic numbers, as in Root's edition and in Skeat's *Index*.[3]

Double rimes occur first in 1 b *Troye joie fro ye*. Later come *tolis scole is foolys* 91 b; *vices vice is* 99 a. A chance variation in *she is me this* 124 a.

The first of the frequent *-esse* rimes occur in 3 b and 4 a; thirty-six more follow in Book 1, not all of them however on the suffix *-nesse* and not all spondaic. The *yng(e)* rimes begin in 11 a, and are followed by sixteen more, not all of which however are spondaic.

Often the same or similar rimes come in neighboring stanzas, e.g. *displese ese* 4 c, *ese plese* 7 a; *creature nature* 15 c, *nature creature* 17 a; *me thé* 96 a, *be thé* 97 a; *byreve leve* 98 c, *leve preve remeve* 99 b; *wiste liste* 97 c, *triste liste* 99 c; *frenesie dye* 104 c, *litargie plye melodie* 105 b; *see degree parde* 121 b, *be mutabilite the* 122 b; *servyse wyse* 137 c, *wyse service wyse* 138 b, *servyse wyse wyse* 142 b. Particularly interesting are the linkings in Cantus Troili: *so woo* 58 a, *fro two mo* 60 b; *he me adversite* 58 b, *quantite be* 59 c; *he youres be* 61 a, *youres is this iwis* 61 b; *fully I* 60 a, *-ly I* 62 a; *maladie dye* 60 c. On the other hand there is similar linking in 88-90, where there is only conversation: *Pandare care* 88 a, *Pandare fare* 90 a; *wo mo two* 88 b, *so therfro go* 90 b; *-esse*

3. W. W. Skeat, *Rime-Index to Chaucer's Troilus and Criseyde*, Chaucer Society, London, 1891.

88 c and *wisse blisse* 89 c. Something similar occurs in stanzas 137, 138, 142, 143: *bridel ydel* 137 a; *tyde abyde hide* 137 b; *servyse wyse* 137 c, *wyse service wyse* 138 b, *servyse wyse wyse* 142 b; *blyve thryve* 138 c; *be thre* 142 c, *the se* 143 a.

Sometimes the rimes of a single stanza are similar in sound: *Appollo fordo go* 11 b, *sholde nolde* 11 c; *spoken wroken broken* 13 b, *ones bones* 13 c; followed by *allone mone* 14 c, *holde olde tolde* 19 b, *noon goon* 19 c; *and olde holde* 23 c. *Hadde madde* 69 a, *spedde dredde* 69 c; *-ence* 74 b, *-aunce* 74 c; *preyinge deyinge* 82 b, *deye seye* 82 c; *speche seche eche* 127 b, *strecche wrecche* 127 c; *falle alle* 150 a, *faste laste laste* 150 b. At the end of Book 1 note *founde stounde* 153 a; *down leoun* 154 a; *stounde wownde* 156 a; and *soore moore loore* 156 b, *cure aventure* 156 c.

Many of these echoes are as the chances fall; some, as in the Cantus, must be deliberate; others a matter of convenience or mechanical repetition; others determined or required by the content. However caused or explained, they add a kind of continuity to the flow of sound.

In Book 11, all the rimes of stanza 8 contain a *d*: *glade made, rede mede sprede* ($\bar{e}^2$), and *bitidde thrydde*. In the next stanza all have an -*e* sound: *speche teche, keene greene teene* ($\bar{e}^1$), and *wente wente*. In stanza 14 the a-rimes are *bet let* and the c-rimes *leere here*. In stanza 15 the rimes are *seyde deyde, rede, dede, rede,* and *telle helle*. (For the run of nine consecutive rimes in -*ede*, five e^2 and four e^1 in Anel see p. 100 below.) In stanza 61 the a-rimes are *feste beheste* and the b-rimes *cas allas Pallas* (repeating the *s* sound), and the c-rimes *purveye deye* echo the c-rimes of the preceding stanza *repreve leve*. In stanza 63 the c-rimes are *seye deye*, and the c-rimes of stanza 66 are *seye pleie*. In stanza 73 the a- and b-rimes have the same consonant but a different vowel: *smyle while* and *telle welle dwelle*.

In Book 111 stanza 39 the a-rimes are *hire* [*here*] *swere* and the c-rimes *deere yfeere*. In stanza 235 the b-rimes are *bere here stere* and the c-rimes are *Pandare care* (with the same consonant).

In Book iv stanza 208 the a- and b-rimes have the same consonant and all three have *e*: *deere yfeere, stere beere ledere, drede strede*.

In Book v stanza 32, the a- and b-rimes are *dere cleere, where were teere*. In the opening stanzas of this Book the rimes make a kind of pattern. The b- and c-rimes of the first stanza and the b-rimes of the second have *n*; the a- of the first, the b- of the second, and the a- and b-rimes of the third all have *e* (e^1 and e^2); the c-rimes of the second and the third and the a- and b-rimes of the fourth all have *-r-, loore more, forlore more bifore*, with *o* again in the c-rimes, *joie Troie*. And so on. Examples of such repetitions may be collected ad lib. Often there seems to be no special reason for them, and after all the permutations are somewhat limited.

Another kind of repetition occurs in Book I, stanza 60, where *-ly I* are the a-rimes and the c-rimes are *-die dye*; and in Book IV, stanza 17, the a-rimes are *lye -mye* and the b-rimes are *-ly -ly by*; and so in v, 38 *-ly -ly* and *-sie folie drye*; and III, 27 *eyen dyen* and *hye -fie -die*.

A special sort of repetition is the echo rime (see above, pp. 37 ff.). It is rather more frequent in the *Troilus* than elsewhere, owing partly to the need of three b-rimes in each of the 1177 stanzas. And for these Chaucer played a few favorites, some of them rather hard. Anyone with a little diligence and the help of Skeat's *Rime-Index* can make his own collection; here a few specimens will suffice. Take first the *-aste* group. This appears first in I, 45 c *caste laste* and then with echo rime in I, 77 b *faste laste laste*. Then this is repeated in I, 150 b, 2, 125 b; and in 2, 129 b *faste faste tagaste*. In 2, 167 b note *faste faste caste*. The following combinations may be noted:

faste laste caste	6 times
faste caste	4 "
faste laste	3 "
faste paste	once
faste thraste	once
laste caste	4 times
laste paste	once
caste paste	once

In 3, 114 c *Horaste laste* is a welcome variation. Another favorite is *-eche*: four times each in Books I and IV, seven times in Book II, six times in Book III, and ten times in Book V; altogether

speche biseche	12 times
speche seche	3 "
speche seche eche	2 "
speche seche leche	2 "
speche eche biseche	2 "
speche preche teche	once
speche preche leche	once
speche preche	2 times

Still another favorite are the *-ace* rimes beginning with *pace grace* 6 c; later (and usually in the end couplets: 53 c, 102 c, 128 c, 130 b, 138 a, 152 c, 154 c.). Altogether *grace* is rimed with *place* 8 times, with *pace* 6 times, with *space* 4 times, with *trespace* once, with *purchace* once. Further *place pace* 3, *place face* 3, *place arace* 1, *place embrace* 1; *grace place face* 3, *grace place chase* 2, *grace place pace* 1, *grace place arace* 1, *grace place purchace* 1; *place face space* 1, *place face pace* 1, *pace deface face* 1, *pace deface* 1, *space face* 1, *space Stace* 1.

Besides the echo rimes in the above lists, Book I has *wise wise* in 138 b, and again in 142 b. Book II has *wente wente* stanza 9, *wise wise* stanza 131, *lay lay* stanza 132, *here here* stanza 235 repeated in 251. Book III has *sike syke* in stanza 9 and *yerne yerne* in stanza 22. In Book IV, stanza 62 has *deyde deyde*. In Book V, stanza 3 *rede rede* and stanza 4 *more more*; and stanza 140 the quite exceptional *was was*, inasmuch as there is no discernible difference between the two.

To these may be added such rimes as *fare feldefare* 3 123; *perturbe disturbe* 4 81, *throwe overthrowe* 4 55, *deface face* 5 131, *byseche seche* 5 162.

Most remarkable of all the rimes in the *Troilus* is the continual repetition of *Troye joie*—thirty times, beginning in the very first stanza and running like a pedal point throughout the poem. It is found three times in Book I, four times in Book II, six times each in Books III and IV, and—ironically—eleven times in Book V. Twenty-two of these are in the closing couplet of the stanzas;

five are a-rimes, and only three are b-rimes (with *fro ye* 1 1, *anoye* 4 187, *tacoye* 5 112). And these are the only rimes on this sound in the poem.[4]

5. STANZAIC FORMS

IF the consensus of scholars be accepted, Chaucer's first stanzaic poems are ABC and Compleynt unto Pite, say, 1369-71. ABC is a free rendering of a part of Guillaume de Deguilleville's *Pèlerinage de la Vie Humaine* in twelve-line octosyllables riming *aabaabbbabba*. For his version Chaucer chose a different stanza *ababbcbc*[5]; and this he used later in the balades Fortune, Rosemounde, Compleynt of Venus (see below), in Former Age (where the seventh stanza, however, goes *ababbcb*), in Bukton, and in MkT. It is sometimes called the Monk's (Tale) stanza. It would be familiar to Chaucer from the French poets, with whom it had become habitual for the balade, usually however with octosyllabic lines.[1] The division into two quatrains is followed by Chaucer as it suits his matter, but as often as not the repetition of b-rimes makes for a continuous unit. Actually the full stops come where the sense requires. In MkT this stanza comes in groups, from a single stanza up to ten (Sampson), eleven (Nero), sixteen (Zenobia). Across the Channel Otes de Graunson was the first to use the stanza in long poems.

Chaucer's only other eight-line stanza is in the so-called Complaint of Venus, a triple balade from Otes de Graunson, with the scheme *ababbccb*[5]. To this Chaucer has added his own Envoy of ten lines *aabaabbaab*[5], with a bow to Graunson as *flour of hem that make in Fraunce*. Chaucer's only other ten-line stanza is in Compleynt to his Lady: nine stanzas (lines 40-127) *aabaabcddc*[5].

Chaucer has two nine-line stanzas, the Compleynt in Mars: sixteen stanzas *aabaabbcc*[5], and Womanly Noblesse, three stanzas

4. The same rimes appear together also in BD 325/26, 1065/66, 1119/20; in HF 155/56, 1471/72; in LGW 1104/05, 1150/51, 1252/53 (all in Dido); and in SqT F 547/48.

1. Henri Chatelain, *Le vers français au XVᵉ siècle*, Paris, 1907, pp. 91-94.

aabaabbab[5] with the same rimes throughout. This latter stanza is used also in Anelida's compleynt (see below).

All these eight- and ten-line stanzas embrace the whole range of Chaucer's writing, from ABC to Bukton. But apart from MkT (97 stanzas) they were occasional rather than staple or favorite patterns.

By all odds Chaucer's favorite stanza is that called, after King James I's *Kingis Quhair*, rime royal, *ababbcc*[5], of which he wrote more than 1800, ranging from Pite at the beginning to the late Truth and Purse.[2] In France of the fourteenth and fifteenth centuries this was "fort cultivé" (Chatelain, p. 144), usually with a proverb in the closing couplet; and there are examples in decasyllables among the balades of Machaut and Deschamps which Chaucer may have seen. But whether he took it from France or adapted it for himself by omitting the fourth b-rime from the MkT stanza has been disputed and no positive statement can be made. Either origin is plausible.

By the same token it is impossible to say whether his five-stress couplet—of which he composed more than 8600—is an extension of the short four-stress couplet familiar to him in RR and used by him in two poems—comprising together 1746 couplets, as well his version of part of the *Roman de la Rose*; or whether it was taken from the rime royal stanza, which ends with two couplets, or from one of the other stanzas which already contained couplets either at the beginning or in the middle. Certainly Chaucer's was the first use of it in English and it has

2. The largest number is of course in the Troilus (1177), then ClT (160), MLT (152), PF (98), down to the single stanza addressed to Adam Scrivener. The theoretical division is, frons: ab (first *pes*), ab (second *pes*), and *cauda* bcc; and this occurs occasionally in Chaucer, e.g., Pite st. 2. For some statistics, see G. H. Cowling, "A Note on Chaucer's Stanza," *R.E.S.* ii (1926), 311-17, with an attempt to show that *Tr.* v, PF, Proem to Mars, PriorT, and MLT iii were written c. 1380 or after, whereas *Tr.* i-iv, ClT, etc. came before 1378. This was disputed by Julia E. Lineberger, *MLN* xlii (1927), 229-31. Obviously a great deal depends on what constitutes a pause or "half-pause" and everything depends on the content of the stanza. In fact, Cowling quotes Egerton Smith, *Principles of English Metre*, Oxford, 1923, p. 244: "Chaucer, if he divided the stanza at all, did so at whatever point suited him best."

been credited to him as an invention.[3] But his first use of it was not, as is commonly said, in LGW but in KtT. For in the Prologue to LGW we learn that Chaucer had written of *al the love of Palamon and Arcite* (F 420, G 408) and hardly anyone now believes that the early version of KtT was in stanzas.

Most of the rime royal stanzas have feminine rimes throughout. None has masculine rimes throughout, but often the first five lines have masculine rimes. In Troilus I nearly 10 per cent of the stanzas are of this kind, in II just over 10 per cent, in IV a little over 10 per cent, and V about 13 per cent. In ClT nearly 20 per cent of the stanzas are of this kind, and in MLT 24 per cent.

For other stanzas there are:

An experimental use of *terza rima* in Compleynt to his Lady, a group of four pieces, as usually printed, the second and third of which rime [a]ba bcb cdc dc[d], [ab]a bcb cdc ded efe fgfg. (Skeat has obligingly supplied the missing lines.)

Single quatrains *abab*[4] in Two Proverbs (among the Doubtful poems).

One five-line stanza *aabba*[5] in Envoy to Purse.

Six six-line stanzas *ababcb*[5] (with the same rimes throughout; i.e., twelve a-rimes, eighteen b-rimes, and six c-rimes) in Lenvoy de Chaucer following the ClT.

Two songs in BD. The first is called a *rym* of *ten vers or twelve* (463), *a maner song* (471) and runs to eleven lines riming *aabba aabaab*[4]. (Different editors have filled out the first part to make an even six lines.) The other is in simple couplets, *aabbaa* (1175-80).

Four roundels: that at the close of PF *abbabAB abbABB*[5]; and the triple roundel, Merciles Beaute (also among the Doubtful poems), with the same pattern.

Sir Thopas is in the tail-rime stanza, with a remarkable number of variations. There are thirty-one stanzas in all, plus the unfinished one at the end (*Namoore of this*, said the Host). The

---

3. Cf. Miss Hammond's tart but sensible observation: "Given a man of great artistic ability, as was Chaucer, and the passage from the familiar four-beat couplet through the five-beat line to the writing of five-beat couplets is not so difficult as to require explanation" (p. 493).

staple is $aa^4b^3aa^4b^3$. In eight stanzas (18, 23, 24, 26, 28-31) the rime of the second couplet is changed: $aa^4b^3cc^4b^3$; and since these multiply towards the end it looks as if Chaucer's enthusiasm was running down. The twelfth stanza is ambiguously $aa^4b^3aa^4b^3$ or $aa^4b^3cc^4b^3$, which is part of the fun.[4] For extra measure and to enhance the fun, in five stanzas Chaucer includes something like the wheel-and-bob device: st. 14 goes $aa^4b^3c^1bb^4c^3$; st. 15 goes $aa^4b^3aa^4b^3c^1aa^4c^3$; st. 16 goes $aa^4b^3aa^4b^3c^1dd^4c^3$; st. 17 goes $aa^4b^3cc^4b^3d^1cc^4d^3$ (unless possibly *thee* and *fay* are meant to rime); st. 27 goes $aa^4b^3cc^4b^3d^1ee^4d^3$.[5]

In LGW, Prologue F 422-23, G 410-11, the poet pleads that he has written many hymns—*balades, roundels, virelayes*—for Love's holy days; and Lydgate in the Prologue to his *Falls of Princes* echoes this: "balades roundels virelaies." Early definitions of the virelay differ a good deal and Chaucer may have used the term loosely. Those which he made for Love's hymnal have disappeared—like the *many a leccherous lay* mentioned in the Retraction. (Skeat, 1, 536 regarded Anel 256-71, 317-32 as virelays, apparently because of the reversed rime scheme.)

There are eleven balades, plus two more of doubtful authenticity: Fortune—a triple balade, nine stanzas $ababbcbc^5$, each group of three having its own rimes; with an envoy $ababbab^5$, the a-rime repeating the b-rime of the preceding group, and with a new b-rime. Rosemounde—three stanzas of eight lines, $ababbcbc^5$; no envoy. Compleynt of Venus—a triple balade, nine stanzas

4. The point is whether *was gras* B 1968/69 are meant to rime with *plas solas* B 1971/72. Kölbing (Manly apparently approving) assumed that *place grace* in the second stanza were meant to rime with *solas Thopas* of the first stanza, and so made the first two stanzas into a special variation going $aa^4b^3aa^4b^3cc^4b^3cc^4b^3$. Both Kölbing and Manly regarded $aa^4b^3cc^4b^3$ as the "standard" form of the stanza, in spite of the fact that Chaucer begins with $aa^4b^3aa^4b^3$ and uses it fifteen times to eight of the other. See Manly, "The Stanza-Forms of *Sir Thopas*," MPh VIII (1910), 141-44. There is another ambiguity in the eighth stanza (B 1944 ff.), where *forest best* (e^1) may be meant to rime with *est almost* (e^2).

5. This is most familiar in *Gawain and the Green Knight*. Chaucer would certainly have seen in it Sir Tristrem (in the Auchinleck MS), which goes $ababababc^3b^1c^3$, and in *Beves of Hamtoun*, some of whose stanzas go $aa^4b^1cc^4b^1$.

ababbccb[5], with an envoy *aabaabbaab*[5]. Truth—three stanzas in rime royal, with a special envoy in the same form. Gentilesse—three stanzas in rime royal; no envoy. Purse—three stanzas in rime royal and an envoy *aabba*[5] without the refrain line. Alceste, in Prologue to LGW—three stanzas in rime royal; no envoy. Doubtful: Against Women Unconstant and Balade of Complaint, each of three stanzas in rime royal, without envoy.

All the balades have the same a-, b-, and c-rimes throughout, with the last line of each stanza repeated as a refrain.

Bukton in the eight-line stanza and Scogan in rime royal both have a final stanza labelled Envoy but are otherwise not balades.

The Compleynt of Anelida in Anel is Chaucer's most gorgeous metrical display. It will be described in Chapter III.

CHAUCER speaks to us, not always distinctly, across the interval of nearly six centuries. But it is fortunate for him that he cannot hear us if we undertake to reply. He would stare and gasp at our pronunciation. When the now eminent Chaucerians read him aloud each goes his own way. Yet, if this is any comfort, the same would be true for Shakespeare and Milton and only a little less so for Browning or Tennyson or Yeats. Just as every poem is in some sense a re-creation by the individual reader of what may be more, or less, akin to the poet's original, so also the sound of his verse is remade by each of us in his own tongue. When we talk of hearing the rhythm of any poet, early or recent, we indulge in a pleasing fallacy. What we hear is our own voices. One has therefore small patience with the offhand advice to students that after a little practice they can *read* Chaucer appreciatively. The intermission of time and the uncertainties of text come beween Chaucer and us and intensify our perplexities. We know too little of the values of pitch and quantity in his speech; and with tone-color we are quite at a loss. We have no way of knowing and little hope of guessing whether he was a timer or a stresser and therefore how much to allow for duration. For instance, what is the effect of *no* in

That no drope ne fille vp on hir brest   A 131

in making up for the lack of a syllable? Or is this a nine-syllable line? Should we pronounce the *-e* of *drope* (A. S. *dropa*) and get ten syllables? As born to the native metric of stress Chaucer may have read his verses with strong accents; but as conscious of and influenced by the syllabism of French and Italian, he may have read them with subdued accent and even, like some modern poets, a kind of singsong or chant.

The prosodist must be prosaic and statistically dull. He accepts his handicap with fortitude. But the poet may rise to the dithyrambic in writing about the same things; may produce the illusion of charm and beauty. Dame Edith Sitwell will perhaps accept the honor of illustration.[1] She has to defend Pope against the perennial charge of monotony. "The reason why," she says, more truly than grammatically, "to an insensitive ear, the heroic couplet seems monotonous is because structure alone, and not texture, has been regarded as the maker of rhythm. In reality, both are the parents of rhythm in poetry; and variations in speed are certainly the result, not only of structure, but also of texture." Too many are deaf to "the infinitely subtle variations and fluctuations of rhythm."

How faint they are [these variations], yet how significant—faint as the little air which comes to us from the feathers of the swan's wings, as he floats upon the lake. How slight and how subtle are the changes of speed, or of depth, due to the difference in texture, and due to the fact that the English, in their cunning over the matter of poetry, have adopted the idea of equivalent syllables, that system which more variation than any other device. . . .

The truth is, that the texture of a poem has, in the past, been regarded as merely a matter of fatness or leaness.

Dame Edith also tells us that she yields to nobody in reverence for Chaucer, though "the bucolic clumsiness of Chaucer's heroic couplets" are not to be compared with "the deep, sleepy richness, like that of some heavily-perfumed dark rose, of Keats' enjambed couplets." Compared with the finesse of cameo detail which is the rewarding achievement of Pope, Chaucer's couplets may be coarse. The tempo of his narrative, even of his descriptions, seldom leaves time for subtleties. He was not a miniaturist. Yet he has occasional passages which deserve our strict attention and which just because they are occasional often escape our notice.

It seemed at first that more practical help would come from the modern school of structural linguistics, with its scientific analysis of the sounds of spoken English. This analysis is presented most clearly in the well-known *Outline of English Structure* by George L. Trager and Henry Lee Smith (1951). Its impingement on metrics may be conveniently found in a series of papers in *The Kenyon Review*, Summer 1956, pp. 411-77, under

1. *Alexander Pope*, London [1930], chap. xviii, "Some Notes on Pope's Poetry," pp. 265 ff.

the general title "English Verse and What it Sounds Like." These papers are by two dedicated linguists, a scholar with advanced views, and by a critic (and poet) who acts as moderator and tries to resolve the differences between old and new.[2] The issue is really the old and fundamental one of prose rhythm *vs*. meter. Arnold Stein's paper, "A Note on Meter" (pp. 451-60) contains the best recent attempt to describe the conflict and cross influence of "the natural rules of language" and stylistic context and the patterns of meter. What *happens* when the elements are melted down and fused makes all the difference, but how a poet manages the process can only be divined, after the fact, by looking closely and wonderingly at the result.

The Trager and Smith analysis of the sounds of English prose, being with its fresh terminology far and away the most thorough and exact hitherto, would seem a very promising start. Its apparatus of symbols affords a better representation of what takes place when prose, or verse, is read aloud than anything hitherto proposed. Yet when it is confronted with the metrical conventions by which all but a few recent poets have composed their verse, it serves mainly to re-emphasize the familiar acknowledged fact that verse is a calculated compromise between prose and meter. Its great value is in revealing, in some degree, how the compromise works, because it displays so clearly the complex prose structures which have to be and are adjusted to the simple pattern of meter. It displays actually the discrepancies to be overcome, but still leaves us to appreciate intuitively how well or ill they are overcome in each instance. It multiplies rather than simplifies our problem. It redoubles the force of Whitehall's brilliant understatement that "Prosody is, in fact, a rather complex subject" (p. 420). For those who are concerned with tone color or "entity" it records thirty-three items of the English phonemic system (nine vowels, three semi-vowels, twenty-one consonants); it finds four degrees of relative stress and four levels of pitch (an element un-

2. For some comments on this symposium see W. K. Wimsatt, Jr. and Monroe C. Beardsley, *PMLA* LXXIV (1959), 585-98; *ibid*. LXXVI (1961), 300-308; also George B. Pace, *ibid*. 413-19.

known to meter), and four kinds of juncture or transition from sound to sound, with and without pause.

The older school however did not altogether miss out with these distinctions; it was only less precise. It recognized that the degrees of stress are almost infinite though it dealt with only three (stress, unstress, and something in between); and surely the Trager and Smith four are arbitrary, a sort of averaging out. It knew enough about pitch but had no good means of handling it. It understood, usually without saying so, that stress is an amalgam of loudness, duration, and pitch all making for some kind of emphasis. Nonetheless, this new analysis is, as Whitehall says, "a work that literary criticism cannot afford to ignore." It illuminates the problems and by rendering them more difficult than they before seemed to be it should lead to a truer appreciation of them and possibly closer to a solution of them.

The theme now is texture: the manifold variations, the enhancements and embellishments which distinguish the language of poetry from the language of prose, the subtle uses (some deliberate, some actually or seemingly accidental) of collocation of vowel and consonantal sounds, the peculiar arrangements of word and phrase which come with the compromise between normal order and the requirements of meter, the shifts and strains of lexical accent to conform with metrical stress, the compression and lengthening of syllables to fit (and more importantly, to notfit) the temporal values implied in the theoretical isochronism of meter—all this and whatever else marks the poet's handling of language and contributes to the beauty of his verse.

Many of these effects are or appear to be mysterious, accessible only to a reader's trained appreciation and therefore obnoxious to analysis. Other effects are fairly recognizable and can be separated and partially described; one of these last is alliteration.

Alliteration is akin to rime and in the native Anglo-Saxon versification it is often called initial rime. But in Chaucer and later verse it is an ornament, not a regulative principle and hence belongs here as a prosodic rather than a metrical phenomenon. Chaucer made his Parson speak disapprovingly of alliteration as *rom ram ruf*, a thing out of the unrefined North. (This indicates at the least Chaucer's awareness of the fourteenth-century alliterative revival, whether or not he had read much of the contemporary alliterative verse.) I am, said the Parson, *a Southren man*, but he cared as little for rime, and there he differed from Chaucer.

Chaucer used alliteration as a conscious ornament only here and there. He seldom made it conspicuous, as in

> *Of Thebes with his waste walles wyde,*   A 1331

which he later softened to

> *To Thebes with his olde walles wyde.*   A 1880

There are other examples of *w w w* in A 374, E 1212; and along with *b* in

> *With spere in honde and bigge bowes bente,*
> *Ector and many a worthi wight out wente;*
> *And in the berd. . . .*   *Tr.* IV 39-41

Here and there also are little flourishes like

> *Hyr lyf, hir love, hir lust, hir lord.*   HF 258

In the battle scene of KtT (A 2601 ff.) the alliteration is a deliberate imitation of the Anglo-Saxon long line; and so also in the description of the naval battle in the Cleopatra Legend (LGW 635 ff.). There are also scattered lines which resemble the fourteenth-century forms of the old alliterative line:

> *A shiten shepherde and a clene sheep*   A 504
> *Flemere of feendes out of hym and here*   B 460
> *To ryden for to reysen vp a rente*   D 1390
> *To been yclawed or to brenne or bake.*   D 1731

Several shades or degrees of alliteration can be recognized, although it is not always easy to distinguish them clearly. The most obvious variety is in the set phrases or formulas which belong to the common stock of the language. They are thin worn coins and seldom do much for the style. Such are *looth or leef, foul or fayr, frend or fo, wyde world, freshe floures, seeke and sore, wax and wane, word and werk, lewed and lered,* and many more.

Sometimes the formulas are employed to good effect, as when the the description of the Monk ends with

His palfrey was as broun as is a berye,   A 207

or when we are told that the Knight was *of his port as meke as is a mayde* (A 69). Then there are border-line collocations, similar to but not quite formulaic, which seem to come naturally in their context: *bestes ne no briddes* (E 572), *stille as stone* (A 3472, E 1818, F 171, etc.); and perhaps *seken straunge strondes* (A 13).

Then there are examples which certainly look like artifice, especially when the alliteration is threefold:

My purpos was to Pite to compleyne	Pite 5
Al ful of fresshe floures white and reede	A 90
Wel koude she carie a morsel and wel kepe	A 130
And eek hir wyves wolde it wel assente	A 374
Ful longe were his legges and ful lene	A 591
And stood forth muwet, milde, and mansuete.	*Tr.* v 194

In some of these specimens it will be observed that a small word or unemphatic syllable receives metrical stress from its position in the line, and vice versa by a shift of accent or stress a strong syllable may be metrically weakened. This results in a kind of secondary alliteration. Examples are numerous: *she hadde a fair forheed* A 154; *she may gouerne and gye* B 1286; *a fair forést* B 1944;

And he hente hym despitously agayn	A 4274
Thus ianglen they and demen and deuyse	F 261
And he wol doun descende and doon youre wille	F 323
That my wyl was his willes instrument.	F 568

Although it is easy to push subtlety too hard in such cases, nevertheless an attentive ear will catch the echoing sounds and feel without always recognizing the effect. Note for example the difference between *Holdeth youre heste* (F 1064) and *holden hir biheste* (F 1163). A rather special case is *pecunyal peyne* (D 1314).

Vowel alliteration, which is standard in Anglo-Saxon, is less noticeable in later verse, but note

> *Til bothe the eyr and erthe brende*   HF 954
> *Than wolde the cat wel dwellen in his in.*   D 350

Sometimes alliteration takes the *abab* pattern:

> *Hath in the Ram his half cours yronne.*   A 8

The alliteration may seem to come in clusters:

> *But whooso wol assay hymselve*
> *Whether his hert kan have pite*
> *Of any sorwe, lat hym see me.*
> *Y wreche, that deth hath mad al naked*
> *Of al the blysse that ever was maked,*
> *Yworthe worste of alle wyghtes.*   BD 574-79

There are numerous examples where the alliteration runs over in consecutive lines and seems to unite them:

> *I have gret wonder, be this lyght,*
> *How that I lyve, . . .*   BD 1-2
> *I holde hit be a siknesse*
> *That I have suffred . . .*   BD 36-37
> *Upon my bed I sat upright*
> *And bad oon reche me a book,*
> *A romaunce, and he it me tok*
> *To rede, . . .*   BD 46-48

So HF 569-70, 579-80, 601-2, 606-7, etc. And in the longer line

> *The holy blisful martyr for to seke*
> *That hem hath holpen . . .*   A 17-18
> *At nyght was come into that hostelrye*
> *Wel nyne and twenty . . .*   A 23-24
> *That I was of hir felaweshipe anon*
> *And made forward . . .*   A 32-33
> *His lymes grete his brawnes harde and stronge*
> *His shuldres brode his armes round and longe . . .*   A 2135-36
> *That swymmen ful of smale fishes lighte,*
> *With fynnes rede and skales sylver bryghte.*   PF 188-89

In sum, Chaucer employs alliteration in all its varieties, seldom as a mere ornament laid on for conspicuous effect, often subtly without drawing attention to it. Too much of it, along with rime, would be oppressive. But everywhere, whether obvious or concealed, whether deliberate or accidental, it adds prosodic color and interest.[3]

What may be regarded as an extension of alliterative effects is the use of vowel and consonant harmonies. On the model of Stevenson's famous exhibit (in his essay "On Style in Literature") of the consonantal harmonies in *Antony and Cleopatra* II, ii, 206-9 one may experiment with Chaucer's Truth. First Stevenson:

> *The BARge she sat iN, like a BURNished throNe*
> *BURNt oN the water: the PooP was BeateN gold,*
> *PURPle the sails, and so PERFumed that*
> *The wiNds were lovesick with them.*

So emphasized the pattern is obvious enough. His treatment of the opening lines of 'Kubla Khan' is a little different.

In Xanadu did Kubla Khan	(KANDL)
A stately pleasure dome decree,	(KDLSR)
Where Alph the sacred river ran,	(KANDLSR)
Through caverns measureless to man,	(KANLSR)
Down to a sunless sea.	(NDLS)

3. A little might be gleaned from comparing the alliteration in Chaucer's prose with that in his verse, but from a small sampling little enough results. In the first half of the introductory part of the Astrolabe (his one prose piece which is not translation) there is no alliteration; then about midway comes a small cluster (*lord of this langage, berith and obeith, lewd compilatour of the labour, swerd shal I sleen*); and a bit later two more, well separated (*calculed for a cause, moeving of the mone*). In Boece I, m. I, 1-20 there are some ten examples, of which the most interesting are *delitable ditees* and *vers of wretchidnesse weten my face with verray teres;* and in the following Prose (1-20) there are fewer examples, but noticeable are *heghte of myn heved* and *the hevene with the heghte of here heved;* and *when sche hef hir heved heyer, sche percede the selve hevene.* In IV, p. 5, 1-20 there is but one (*nedy and nameles*), and in the following Metre (1-20) two (*sovereyne centre; moeveth folk, and maketh*). At the beginning of ParsT, where there is something like blank verse, note *comen alle to the knoweleche; wyse; Stondeth up on the weyes, axeth of olde, walketh in that wey, fynde refressehynge, leden, folk to oure lord.* In the first part of the Mel, where blank verse is more prominent, there is very little alliteration. Thus nothing here or elsewhere in his prose suggests that Chaucer's ear cherished alliteration for its own sake or avoided it when it came naturally.

Now Chaucer:

> *Flee fro the prees, and dwelle with sothfastnesse,*
> *Suffyce unto thy good, though it be smal;*
> *For hord hath hate, and climbing tikelnesse,*
> *Prees hath envye, and wele blent overal;*
> *Savour no more than thee bihove shal;*
> *Reule wel thyself, that other folk canst rede;*
> *And trouthe thee shal delivere, it is no drede.*

One notes first the alliteration of *Fle suffyce folk* and *sothfastnesse Savour* and *hord hath hate bihove* and *wele Werk wel* and *climbing canst* and *over- other*. One notes also the number of *l*'s, though only one, *delivere*, is metrically stressed: *Fle dwelle smal climbing tikelnesse wel blent overal shal -self folk shal*. Perhaps one should note also the *r*'s in *prees hord Prees overal Savour more Werk other rede Trouthe drede*. In the same fashion one may examine the vowels: $\bar{e}^1$, $\bar{e}^2$, $\breve{e}$ in the first line; $\breve{e}$, $\bar{e}^2$ in the sixth; $\bar{\imath}, \breve{\imath}$ in the second, third, and fourth lines, and a sprinkling of *o* throughout the stanza.

> *Tempest thee noght al croked to redresse,*   (TRD)
> *In trust of hir that turneth as a bal:*   (TR)
> *Gret reste stant in litel besinesse;*   (STR)
> *Be war also to sporne ayeyns an al;*   (SP)
> *Stryve not, as doth the crokke with the wal.*   (STRND)
> *Daunte thyself, that dauntest otheres dede;*   (SD)
> *And trouthe thee shall delivere, it is no drede.*   (TRND)

Here the *s*, *t*, and *d* stand out clearly. Both in alliteration and in unemphatic positions (like *l* in the preceding stanza). Among the vowels *e* is the most prominent.

But how much of all this is accidental and how much is significant each reader will decide for himself. The song of Troilus at the end of Book III will repay similar study.[4]

It is well known that the search for rimes may produce felicitous results, and sometimes the opposite. Chaucer illustrates both

4. The curious will want to see the work of J. R. Firth, "Modes of Meaning," in *Essays and Studies*, N.S. IV (1951), 119-49, with further references.

kinds. In *Tr.* II 1382-84 Pandarus makes a curious slip in the heat
of his argument. The *happy fallying strook* which brings down
the sturdy ook happily echoes the sense and the oak falls heavily

> *As don thise rokkes. . .*

but then, needing a rime for *nones* and *ones,* he (Chaucer) adds
to our surprise

> *or thise milnestones.*

The perennial garden of the Parlement Chaucer describes as

> *Upon a ryver, in a grene mede, . . .*
> *With floures white, blewe, yelwe, and rede,*
> *And colde welle-stremes, nothing dede.*　　　PF 184-87

The last phrase may be charitably taken as 'living waters,' but it
looks very much like padding. Then a few stanzas later:

> *Whan every foul cometh there to chese his make, . . .*
> *And that so huge a noyse gan they make*
> *That erthe, and eyr, and tre, and every lake. . .* PF 310-13

The echo rimes *make make* are supplemented by an unexpected
topographical detail, for there had been no hint of lakes in the
landscape. The nearest was only *welle-stremes.* (In twelve of the
fourteen manuscripts the scribes wrote *see* for *eyr,* thus further
extending the picture!) When Griselda's child is taken from her
she assures Walter that

> *No lengthe of tyme or deth may this deface*
> *Ne chaunge my corage to another place;*　　　E 510-11

and when her children are restored to her,

> *with hir salte teres*
> *She bathed bothe hir visage and hir heres.*　　　E 1084-85

At the end however Chaucer atones brilliantly: the rime gave him
a fresh vivid metaphor for the death of the aged Janicula:

> *His wyues fader in his court he kepeth*
> *Till that the soule out of his body crepeth.*　　　E 1133-34

And in the Legend of Dido the rime seems to have brought with
it a happy (albeit not original) phrase:

Into the court the houndes been ybrought;
And upon coursers, swift as any thought.   LGW 1194-95

An examination of Chaucer's riming habits may be fruitful in other ways. For example, the word *degre* is recorded seventy-five times in the Concordance and in all but a few instances it occurs in rime. The word *cas* occurs seventeen times in LGW, and twelve of these are in rime. The word *twelve* occurs eighteen times in rime, all with *-selve*; and twelve times in these eighteen it stands first. This distinction is of course not conclusive, but it suggests that the notion of 'twelve' was usually first in his mind and called for the only answering rime available.[5] In the other six instances, where *twelve* stands second, one can only say that the order is natural. In four instances the numerical sense of the word is paramount: BD 831/32, A 527/28, G 1002/03 (the twelve Apostles), and *Tr.* II 106/08 (the twelve books of the *Thebaid*). In three instances the reference is to time: BD 573/74, *Tr.* II 1399/1400 (twice twelve hours or a day), and BD 1323/24 (the clock struck twelve or midnight). In D 1967/68 it is a matter of dividing a farthing into twelve parts. In the other nine instances *twelve* is used as a round number: A 4141/42 (ten or twelve feet from the bed), F 383/84 (ten or twelve women with Canace), BD 419/20 (the trees are ten or twelve feet apart), BD 463/64 (the knight's song has ten or twelve verses (actually eleven!), *Tr.* V 97/98 *tymes twyes twelve*, *Tr.* V 923/24 *be kyng of Greces twelve*, *Tr.* IV 400/02 *fairer than swiche twelve*, HF 1215/16, 2125/26 *many (a) thousand tymes twelve*. It is therefore reasonable to suppose that in BD 723 *twelve* stands for a round number, say, a dozen. There the dreamer, comforting the knight's despair, says:

Thogh ye had lost the ferses twelve,
And ye for sorwe mordred yourselve,

you would be condemned like earlier suicides and others who died for love. These *ferses twelve* have proved a difficulty. Skeat made

5. There are two exceptions, for twice he rimes *-selve* with *delve*, once in the description of the Plowman (A 535/36) where *delve* is natural, and once in FrkT where Canace delves for herbs to heal the falcon-princess (F 637/38). In both instances *-selve* comes first.

an unconvincing arithmetical computation; Robinson seems to
think they would be all a player's pieces except the king, and
adds: "But the use of *fers* for 'piece in general' is difficult." Professor Cooley (*MLN* LXIII (1948), 30-35) proposed as a drastic
solution to omit the article, thus leaving a seven-syllable line with
unusual rhythm, and understanding *ferses twelve* as by metonomy
twelve games—"though you had lost twelve queens, i.e., twelve
games." A simpler textual solution would be to read *of* for *the*,
i.e., though you had lost a dozen *ferses*.

Several of Chaucer's ways of varying the strictly iambic line
have been already illustrated: trochaic and spondaic substitution,
the omission of a syllable at the head of a line, or occasionally in
its middle (Lydgate), and such modifications as may result from
elision, the slurs, and hiatus. There are other methods to be
described presently, but first a final word on the trisyllabic foot.
This was left (p. 22) as a matter not to be proved or disproved,
but received or rejected on subjective grounds, a choice between
doctrinaire rigor and artistic design. Granted that most lines can
be compressed or expanded by elision etc. to a theoretical ten (or
eight) syllables, it is still a question whether Chaucer read them
so, with ten syllables as the governing principle, or whether he
allowed for a possible extra syllable (as later poets have nearly
always done) as one of the most natural ways of varying the
formal regularity of a series of iambs. In a word, how far should
the modern reader go in welcoming his kind of variation?

Professor Donaldson says cautiously (*op. cit.*, p. 1108) that
"anapestic substitution in Chaucer on a large scale is difficult to
prove." How large is a large scale? Even Swinburne, a master of
the anapest with iambs in lyric measures, uses it sparingly in the
heroic line. One may accept

My lady cometh, that all this may disteyne	LGW F 255
To swich as hym thynketh able for to thryve	*Tr.* II 207
If thow louest thy self thow louest thy wyf	E 1385
Yet putteth he in hyt such mysaventure	Mars 229

and many other such lumpy contractions; even

Up to the holughnesse of the eighte spere,	*Tr.* V 1809

which is not helped much by adopting the usual spelling *holow-nesse*. One may explain

> *And with my couerchief couered my visage*   D 590

as pointing ahead to 'kerchief,' though the word is never so spelled in the manuscripts. One may manage such slurs and contractions as in

> *And lyk a fissher, as men alday may se*   Mars 237
> *And in hire bosom down the lettre he thraste* *Tr.* II 1155
> *Or at the leste I love hire as wel as ye,*
> *And lenger have served hire in my degre*   PF 452-53
> *That bad men sholde wed his similitude*   A 3228
> *That ye mowe haue a suffisant perdoner.*   C 932

But there are still

> *And saugh his visage al in another kynde*   A 1401
> *Myn is the stranglyng and hangyng by the throte* A 2458
> *Seuene hennes for to doon al his plesaunce*   B 4056
> *Pekke hem vp right as they growe and ete hem in* B 4157
> *The moore it brenneth the moore it hath desyr*   D 374
> *A likerous mouth moste han a likerous tayl*   D 466
> *As wel of that as of othere thynges moore*   D 584
> *Where is youre fader o Grisildis he sayde*   E 297
> *That whelpes eten somme of the crommes alle*   G 60
> *With the nones that he hadde owher a wif*   LGW 1540

(Skeat recommends that we say *With th' nones*), and many others. One of Chaucer's clearest examples is

> *And al foryive, while that I lyve may*   Anel 280

with the internal rimes *-yive lyve*: *lyve* must have two syllables and to match it so must *-yive*. In

> *The ordre of compleynt requireth skylfully*   Mars 155

is the ear happy, or the tongue, with *Th'ordr'of* as a disyllabic foot? Is it better in

> *As wel in cristendom as in hethenesse*   A 49

to squeeze *cristendom* down to two syllables; or in

Wyd was his parisshe and houses fer asonder   A 491

to squeeze *parisshe* down to one syllable, than to welcome the
anapest? Or in

And wonderly delyuere and of greet strengthe   A 84

should one make *delyuere* a mere iamb? Which makes a better
line

For hym was leuerẹ haue át his beddes heed   A 293

or

For hym was leuerẹ háue at his beddes heed?
And finally in

And specially from euery shires ende   A 15

consider the emphasis gained by giving *specially* and *euery* their
full syllabic value. Compare *to Caunterbury they wende* (A 16)
and *my pilgrymage To Caunterbury* (A 21-22) with

That toward Caunterbury wolden ryde.   A 27

The first two have a slight suggestion of eagerness if the four
syllables of *Caunterbury* are a little hurried, while in the last,
where all four syllables have to be sounded, the whole line is
slowed and attention drawn, with a special emphasis on *toward*,
to the simple fact that the Pilgrims were setting out *toward
Caunterbury*. No more is promised: they might never arrive.

Such subtleties are not beyond Chaucer's scope, though they
may not be very common, and they should not be neglected.

Among the other devices employed by Chaucer for metrical
variety four may be distinguished:

1. the deliberate use of irregular lines, which do not easily conform to the theoretical scansion;

2. the use of enjambement to subordinate the line unit to the
syntactic context;

3. the placing of grammatical or rhythmical pauses at regular
or varied positions; and

4. the different weighting of (consecutive) lines.

1. Many examples of the irregular line will be noted in the Appendix on CYP and T. A few others are here added. There is always the risk that what looks like irregularity may be due to a faulty text. There is always the possibility that now and then Chaucer, what with carelessness or even indifference, or owing to the interruptions of a busy life, left a line imperfect. But there must also be lines of a calculated irregularity—Milton is a master of this practice—to rouse a reader or listener and by its opposite enhance the formal pattern. Now he would be rash indeed who would venture always to decide under which category any particular line should be placed; one can only invoke what Matthew Arnold liked to call tact.

The KtT has several peculiar lines, which fit in with other evidences of an early date (the pre-CT version) or may illustrate Chaucer's feeling for meter when he composed the poem; e.g.,

Of the goddesse clateren faste and rynge	A 2359
Whan that thow vsedest the beautee	2385
I am yong and vnkonnyng as thow woost	2393
Myn be the trauaille and thyn be the glorie	2406
Gyggynge of sheeldes with layners lasynge	2504
That shal been ordeyned on either syde	2553
That is to seyn trouthe honour knyghthede.	2789

For some early examples take

Under the cros, ne his greevous penaunce	ABC 82
Ne advocat noon that wol and dar so preye	102
Zacharie yow clepeth the open welle	177
Algate my spirit shal nevere dissevere;	Pite 115

and from the probably early MancT

Hath naturelly set in a creature	H 162
Or leest of reputacioun that wol she take	185
And a poure wenche oother than this	215
To Alisandre was told this sentence	226
Dissimule as thow were deef if that thow here.	347

From the *Troilus* one could gather a good many specimens in

which the meter and the natural rhythm do not 'incorporate,'
e.g.—

> *So aungelik was hir natif beaute*   I 102
> *Al were it wist, but in pris and up born*   375
> *To nevere no man, for whom that he so ferde*   739
> *And yit mathinketh this avaunt masterte*   1050
> *And that she sholde han his konnyng excused*   II 1079
> *As licour out of a lambyc ful faste*   IV 520
> *That I am as out of this world agon*   780
> *Was nevere or that day wist at any feste*   V 441
> *Strof love in hire ay, which of hem was more*   819
> *To warmen of the est see the wawes weete*   1109

(so Root, Robinson, and most MSS; but Globe has *To warme of
th'este*). In SumT there is a very odd line,

> *A goddes hal peny or a masse peny* [*:any*]   D 1749

which can be scanned either by taking the third foot *peny or* as
trochaic substitution with elision, or by taking *peny or* as a
weak third foot—perhaps anticipating the modern pronunciation
[hapni]. The compound *hal peny* does not occur elsewhere in
Chaucer.

Spondaic substitution may lead to peculiar effects. Compare

> *Ther was no man no wher so vertuous*   A 251
> *Ther was no dore that the he nolde heue of harre,* A 550

which are plain enough, with

> *Of studie took he moost cure and moost heede,*   A 303

in which the first *moost* occupies the stressed position and the
second the unstressed. In

> *Ne noon so grey goos goth ther in the lake*   D 269

there is properly only one spondaic foot but the emphatic monosyllables intensify the effect. There is a notable balance in the
nine-syllable line

> *Som this som that as hym liketh shifte*   D 104

and a very special effect is gained by the monosyllabic first foot
and inversion of the second in

> *Who peynted the leoun tel me who;*   D 692

and in

> *That with a sherte his lyf les*   HF 1414

there is a still different, and amusing, use of the spondaic foot. In

> *In crepeth age alwey as stille as stoon*   E 121

it is grammatical inversion which produces the spondaic first
foot.

> *To pleyes of myracles and of mariages*   D 558

does not seem right. Some MSS, and some editors, read *and to
mariages*, but this does not help the scansion. Skeat and Koch
omit the second *of*. Striking also are

> *Many a bright helm, and many a spere and targe,*
> *Many a fresh knyght, and many a blysful route.*   Anel 33-34

Perhaps there is inversion of both the third foot and the
fourth in

> *No thyng forgat he the care and the wo.*   D 727

So Robinson, without comment, and Manly, who however says
(III, 459): "The textual situation here is very puzzling." Nearly
all the MSS of his cd group have *the penaunce and wo;* so also
Skeat and Globe. But El Hg and others have *the sorowe and wo.*
It looks as though Chaucer left an unpolished line and the scribes
did what they could with it.

2. In the sixteenth century, English verse, especially the five-
stress line, seems to have started all over again with awkward
stiffness—as though Chaucer had never been. The extraordinary
flexibility of Chaucer's line had dwindled, owing to the changes
in the language, to the "roughness of a Scotch tune" so that his
easy freedom stands out as something to wonder at. He had shown
the way, but south of Tweed the way was lost. Chaucer, however,
it is worth remembering, began slowly. In ABC and Pite most

of the lines end with a pause, though there are notable exceptions
—some dozen in ABC:

> *that with good entente*
> Axeth thin helpe   11-12
> *a greevous accioun*
> Of verrey right   20-21
> *which than nevere*
> Were bitter   49-50
> *that Moyses wende*
> Had ben a-fyr   93-94
> *sith thou canst and wilt*
> Ben to the seed of Adam   181-82

and so on. In Pite

> *to compleyne*
> Upon the crueltee   5-6
> *do youre myght*
> To helpe Trouthe.   73-74

And in the couplets of MancT

> *of victorie*
> Of Phitoun   H 127-28
> *a likerous appetit*
> On lower thing   189-90
> *doon any execucion*
> Vp on youre ire   287-88
> *hath rakel ire*
> Fully fordoon   289-90

and half a dozen more.

Soon, however, run-on lines become frequent and the couplet
is subordinated to the sentence movement. Sometimes the two
lines go together:

> *A YEMAN hadde he and seruants namo*
> *At that time for hym liste ryde so.*   A 101-02
>
> *Fair was this mayde in excellent beautee*
> *Abouen euery wight that man may see.*   C 7-8

couplet may be divided between two sentences:

> *And he was clad in coote and hood of grene.*   A 103
> *A sheef of pecok arwes bright and kene*   A 104
>
> *To heren of his clere voys the soun.*   H 115
> *Certes the kyng of Thebes Amphioun.*   H 116

Or the couplet may stand by itself, closed, or two or more couplets may run together. In the eleven couplets of the description of the Squire (A 79-100) six are closed, two are grouped together, one is divided into single lines; and the first two divide after the third line. The description of the Friar begins with the second line of a couplet. In narrative, where the sentences tend to be longer—although they are often short and loosely joined by *And*—the same freedom obtains. In A 994-97 there are four successive run-on lines.

In stanzas likewise the breaks run through the riming groups in all possible combinations. Sometimes the *abab* quatrain of the rime royal stanza is held together, as in E 64-67, E 148-51, E 519-22. Or the middle couplet may stand by itself, as in E 116-17. Less often than one might expect the final couplet forms a unit, as in E 335-36, E 377-78. The last two couplets may run together, as in E 438-41. Sometimes the whole stanza forms a unit, as in E 197-203, E 253-59; or two stanzas may run together

> *Vpon hir cheere he wolde hym often auyse*   E 238
> *Commendynge in his herte hir wommanhede.*   E 239

The principal pause rarely falls at the end of the first line, as in E 365, *Tr.* 1 99; but sometimes after the second line, as in E 338. Quite unusual is the stanza

> *The sergeant goth and hath fulfild this thyng.*
> *But to this markys now retourne we.*
> *For now goth he ful faste ymagyngng*
> *If by his wyves cheere he myghte se—*
> *Or by hir word aperceyue—that she*
> *Were chaunged. But he neuere hir koude fynde*
> *But euere in oon ylike sad and kynde.*   E 596-602

[The punctuation is here mine.]

The *Troilus* abounds in every kind of variation. The bidding prayer (1 22-51) is a single loose sentence of thirty-one lines, with asides and parentheses—one long breath of four stanzas running over into the fifth. Run-on stanzas are frequent throughout; to say nothing of three consecutive stanzas beginning with *And* in one of Pandarus' long speeches (1 967, 974, 981). As soon as the Proem to Book 1 is finished and the narrative begins there is a remarkable subordination of metrical to rhetorical rhythm:

> *It is wel wist how that the Grekes stronge*
> *In armes, with a thousand shippes, wente*
> *To Troiewardes, and the cite longe*
> *Assegeden;*   1 57-60

which is closely followed by

> *Now fil it so that in the town there was*
> *Dwellynge a lord ...*   1 64
> *That in science so expert was that he*
> *Knew wel ...*
> *   that Troye sholde*
> *Destroyed ben, ...*   1 77

and the next two stanzas (78-91) contain seven run-on lines.

In the short couplet the music is different. The rimes follow each other quickly, leaving less room in the line for special effects or for complete predication. Hence more frequent enjambement, fewer examples of the line as unit. Hence also a feeling of rapidity, whether appropriate or not. It is not improbable that Chaucer first learned from the French octosyllabic couplet the values of enjambement and thence adopted it in his longer line.

The BD should be marked *molto allegro*, and if read to this tempo, set by the meter, it becomes, with all its more than thirteen hundred lines, shorter than it looks in print. The poet must have written it with gusto—'elegy' and all—and it has to be perused in the same spirit—

> *This was my sweven; now hit ys doon;*

or rather, if the editors could be weaned of their punctuational ways:

This was my sweven. Now hit ys doon.

The first line which can be regarded as a unit comes only at l. 41:

> *Passe we over untill eft.*
> *That wil not be mot nede be left.*
> *Our first mater is good to kepe.* 41-43

Here also the editors prefer semicolons, but why? The staccato marks the end of his little digression.

Enjambement is everywhere. At the very beginning:

> *I have gret wonder, by this lyght,*
> *How that I lyve, for day ne nyght*
> *I may nat slepe wel nygh noght.*

So ends the first sentence, though the editors prefer a semicolon. And note that it ends midway of the couplet. Then

> *I take no kep*
> *Of nothing* 6-7
> *agaynes kynde*
> *Hyt were to lyven in thys wyse.*
> *For nature wolde nat suffyse*
> *To noon erthly creature*
> *Nat longe tyme to endure*
> *Withoute slep* 16-21
> *Myselven can not telle why*
> *The sothe* 34-35
> *I have lorn*
> *My blysse.* 685-86

It was no doubt in BD that Chaucer first learned to adapt his meter to conversational exchanges; cf. 1042 ff., 1137 ff., 1298 ff.

In HF, which is only 824 lines longer than the BD and seems very much longer, the pace is slower—except in the incomparable Book II with its voluble Eagle. On the whole the meter is smoother; for having learned its ways Chaucer could better show his *art poetical*—almost *with to gret an ese*. The long cataloguing sentence at the beginning is perfectly managed and towards the end there is a remarkable display of *maistrye* in the forty-one *of*

phrases in seventeen lines (1960 ff.), varying from one to three
to the line, the ideas coming mostly in contrasting pairs, a few
without *of*. A little earlier there is a fine display of trailing
parentheses:

> *Loo! how shulde I now telle al thys?*
> *Ne of the halle eke what nede is*
> *To tellen yow that every wal*
> *Of hit, and flor, and roof, and al*
> *Was plated half a foote thikke*
> *Of gold, and that nas nothyng wikke,*
> *But, for to prove in alle wyse,*
> *As fyn as ducat in Venyse,*
> *Of which to lite al in my pouche is?*   1341-49

3. Pauses, not only at the end of a line (or their absence, enjambement), but within the line, are a prime source of rhythmic
variation. They are of course in the first instance grammatical or
rhetorical, but their position is of great importance. They may
occur after the first syllable:

> *First in the temple of Venus maystow se*   A 1918
> *Thoughte: "I shal felen what he mene, ywis;*   Tr. II 387

(so also *Seyde* II 1728; *I, that* IV 493; *So, though* IV 1349); or before the last syllable:

> *And ther with al he bleynte and cride A*   A 1078
> *So cryede, "Kek kek! kow kow! quek quek!" hye;*   PF 499

and in *Troilus*: *quod she, "dere* II 1103; *He seyde: "yis"* II 1424;
answerde: "nay" IV 640; *my deere herte, ye,* IV 1334. There may
be several in one line

> *But now, help God, and ye, swete, for whom*
> *I pleyne, ikaught, ye, nevere wight so faste!*   Tr. I 533-34

(wherein Chaucer treats us to the double use of *ye* and the amusing repetition of *I* and *i-*.).

In LGW 1114-24 (Dido) he has a rhetorical flourish in which
eight of the eleven lines begin with *Ne*. The first, seventh, tenth,
and eleventh lines have no internal pause. In the eighth line the

pause comes after the first foot; in the second and fourth in the
second foot; in the third, sixth, and ninth after the second foot;
and in the fifth after the third foot. Counting syllables, succes-
sively, after 10, 3, 5, 3, 6, 4, 10, 2, 4, 10, 10.

In Book II 344-48 of the *Troilus* Pandarus, trying to convert
Criseyde after having in Book I converted Troilus, becomes lyrical:

> *Wo worth the faire gemme vertules!*
> *Wo worth that herbe also that dooth no boote!*
> *Wo worth that beaute that is routheles!*
> *Wo worth that wight that tret ech undir foote!*

Here the signs are less obvious, but there is a slight pause after
the seventh syllable, then after the sixth, then after the fifth, then
after the fourth (as well as the full stop at the end of each line),
so that each of the three *that* clauses is longer by one syllable than
the one before. Moreover, all four lines start with the spondaic
Wo worth; the negative adjectives in *-les* are varied by the simple
negative *no boote*; and *that* occurs six times in three lines.

The lists of trees (176-82) and birds (337-64) in PF have
consecutive pauses after the second foot:

> *The byldere ok, . . .*
> *The piler elm, . . .*
> *The gentil faucoun, . . .*
> *The kynges hand; . . .*

In *Troilus* II 435-36 the lines are metrically balanced 2 +3,
3 +2.

> *O cruel god! O dispitouse Marte!*
> *O Furies thre of helle! on yow I crye!*

More striking is the series in IV 260 ff., where Troilus is lamenting
over the exchange:

> *Than seyde he thus: "Fortune, allas the while!*
> *What have I don, what have I thus agilt?*

In the seventy-seven lines of this speech the pause comes after the
second foot twenty-six times; and what is more noticeable, in the

forty-nine lines of Pandarus' reply, twenty-three lines have a pause in this same place. Again, in Book v 481-87, where Troilus is impatient to leave Sarpendon's, the seven successive lines have a pause in this same position, and then in 489, 490, 492, 497, 498, etc. What in one place is or may be regarded as a designed artistic effect, may turn into a nearly meaningless pattern or habit. In *Troilus* II 841-47, the third stanza of Antigone's Cantus, there is a capital balance which looks natural and probably came easily but is nontheless effective: the first and fifth lines are each a metrical unit; the second and fourth lines divide (counting syllables) $4 + 6$, the third $5 + 5$, the sixth $2 + 4 + 4$, and the last $6 + 4$.

The grammatical divisions and the metrical are played off against one another in

> *hire brighte face,*
> *Hire lymes lene*   v 708-09

and in

> *Ny nevere saugh a more bountevous*
> *Of hire estat, ne gladder, ne of speche*
> *A frendlyer, na more gracious*
> *For to do wel, ne lasse hadde nede to seche*
> *What for to don.*   I 883-87

The same effect in longer groups is met in: *And some, And som, And som, And some* I 914, 916, 918, 920. Or the natural rhythm may run straight against the theoretical iambs:

> *Al esily, now, for the love of Marte!*   II 988
> *And thow shalt fynde us, if I may, sittynge*
> *At som wyndowe, into the strete lokynge.*   II 1014-15
> *His hed to the wal, his body to the grounde*   IV 244
> *   hard it is*
> *The wolf ful, and the wether hool to have.*   IV 1373-74

Similarly the phrasal balance of $2 + 2$ may be played off against the five iambic beats:

> *For kaught is proud, and kaught is debonaire* I 214
> *So gret desir, and swiche affeccioun;*   I 296

or the two movements appear in direct contrast:

> *And next the valeye is the hil olofte,*
> *And next the derke nyght the glade morwe,*   1950-51

where one line has only four rhetorical stresses and the other the full five iambs. So also two neighboring balanced four-beat lines

> *By nyght or day, for wisdom or folye*   1452
> *Was ay on hire, that fairer was to sene*   1454

are followed in the next stanza by

> *My dere herte, allas! myn hele and hewe,*   1461

where the balanced phrases are brought into the metrical scheme by *allas*. Or the balance may find another variation through a polysyllable:

> *Eke whit by blak, by shame ek worthinesse.*   1642

In this matter of pauses one frequently runs against the modern editorial practices. In

> *He koude rooste and sethe and broille and frye*   A 383

Skeat, Robinson, and Manly (in his 1928 edition) draw attention to the pauses by commas; Globe leaves the reader his own choice. In

> *The holy blisful martir for to seke*   A 17

Skeat, Globe, and Robinson have no commas; Manly one after *holy*. In

> *He was a verray parfit gentil knyght*   A 72

Skeat has no commas; Globe one after *parfit*, Robinson one after *verray*, Manly one after *verray* and one after *parfit*. Just where and how distinct are the pauses in

> *Wel nyne and twenty in a compaignye*
> *Of sondry folk by aventure yfalle*
> *In felaweship and pilgrymes were they alle*
> *That toward Caunterbury wolden ryde?*   A 24-27

The editors differ, of course, and so impose their own notions of the rhythm. But they agree on a comma after *alle*. Again, there is a slight pause—ever so slight, not to be marked by any punctuation, yet felt—in

> *So priketh hem nature in hir corages.* A 11

Nature is made emphatic by the grammatical inversion; the predication is complete; and the concluding phrase is in a sense epexegetical.

It is sometimes said that Chaucer never graduated to the practice of a full stop within the line, that he never began a sentence in the middle of a line. This depends of course on the modern editors. Take for example

> *Ther was also a REUE and a MILLERE . . .*
> *A MAUNCIPLE and my self ther were namo,* A 542, 544

where a semicolon or a dash is usually thought sufficient after *self*, and a period would be better. And there are a great many other examples.

4. Chaucer, like most later poets, varies the line by means of what Miss Hammond has called "weight." This may include balancing an otherwise light or empty line with the extra weight of one or more spondaic feet in a following line, but primarily means the practice of allowing in place of the normal five stresses four, three, or even two rhetorical emphases. This point is discussed in Appendix 1, on the Rhythmic Heresy (pp. 117 ff. below) and touched on incidentally *passim*.

Four-beat lines are common. They may result from parallel phrasing as in

> *Humblest of herte, hyest of reverence,* Pite 57

or from subordinating a secondary accent, as in

> *Honour, estat, and wommanly noblesse,* Tr. 1287

or from the comparative frequency of inflectional endings (as compared with modern English), as in

> *To comen swiftly to that place dere,* PF 76

or quite simply from a number of monosyllables which do well enough to satisfy the iambic pattern but do not really require rhetorical emphasis.

Often it is difficult to decide how many rhythmic beats there
·e in a line. Consider the following scattered examples:

And ben assented when I shall be sleyn	Pite 53
To kepe a shrewe for it wol nat be	H 151
Er ye doon any execucioun	H 287
For to be subgetz and been in seruage	E 482
Or by hir word aperceyue that she	E 600
Where as I was noght worthy for to be	E 829
Now fil it so that in the town there was	Tr. 1 64
She nas nat with the leste of hir stature	Tr. 1 281
And of hir look in him ther gan to quyken	Tr. 1 295
And whan that he in chambre was allone	Tr. 1 358
This Sarpedoun, as he that honourable	Tr. v 435

and a few examples in the talking style of the Wife's Prologue

But that I axe why what the fifthe man	D 21
And to my chambere with inne my bour	D 300
Thou shalt noght bothe thogh thow were wood	D 313
Be maister of my body and of my good	D 314
And for to se and eek for to be seye	D 552
Ther fore I made my visitacions	D 555
By maistrie al the soueraynetee	D 817

and these which are almost certainly two-beat:

Of bigamye or of octogamye	D 33
Of tribulacioun in mariage	D 173
Vpon my youthe and on my iolytee	D 470
To vigilies and to processions	D 556
But for that I was purueyed of a make.	D 591

But the surest way to appreciate Chaucer's variety in this respect is to turn back to the familiar opening paragraphs of the
General Prologue and read them with the natural prose emphases,
leaving the scansion quite in the background. In the first paragraph four lines have the regular five stresses (3, 10, 12, 14);
nine have only four (2, 5, 6, 7, 8, 9, 13, 15, 17); one has three
(16); three might be read as having either three or four (1, 4, 11);
one has only two (18). In the second paragraph there is no line

with the full five stresses; three have four (22, 25, 33); nine have three (20, 23, 26, 28, 29, 30, 31, 32, 34); three might be read as having either three or four (19, 21, 24); one has two or perhaps three (27). In the third paragraph seven of the eight lines have three (35, 36, 37, 38, 40, 41, 42) and one has two (39). Taken altogether in the forty-two lines there are four with the regular five stresses; twelve with four beats; seventeen with three beats; six which might be read with either three or four; and three with two beats. The proportions will naturally vary in different poems; but in the first six stanzas of *Tr.* v there are five lines with the full complement; nineteen with four beats; sixteen with three; two with two. In both passages, it must be emphasized, the figures take account only of the words or syllables which are stressed in a strictly prose rendering, regardless of the metrical pattern. Both passages should be studied closely with attention directed now to the prose rhythm and now to the metrical scheme, and then to both together.

Another way to exhibit Chaucer's variety is to list seriatim these forty-two lines (A 1-42) so measured: 3/4, 4, 5, 3/4, 4, 4, 4, 4, 4, 5, 3/4, 5, 4, 5, 4, 3, 4, 2; 3/4, 3, 3/4, 4, 3, 3/4, 4, 3, 2, 3, 3, 3, 3, 3, 4, 3; 3, 3, 3, 3, 2, 3, 3, 3.

If any conclusion could be drawn from such statistics it would be the not unexpected one that Chaucer handles the line with easy freedom, that he is not bound by metrical regularity or afraid even of a run of four or five lines with the same number of beats. For between two successive four-beat lines—

> *Inspired hath in euery holt and heeth*
> *The tendre croppes and the yonge sonne*   A 6, 7

or two three-beat lines—

> *And shortly whan the sonne was to reste*
> *So hadde I spoken with hem euerichon*   A 30, 31

there are still effective differences of rhythm.

CHAUCER was first of all a narrative poet. His main interest, and ours, is in the story and its adjuncts, the people and their surroundings, which make the story something more than a bald and unconvincing narrative. The 'poetry' is therefore diffused. It is infrequently concentrated into separable parts and passages which, so to say, float the reader over level stretches and at times lift him above them. Yet all narrative poets have liked to heighten the narrative and refresh the reader, here and there, with fine things, purple inlays, which are meant frankly as embellishments. In Chaucer many of these are subdued inconspicuously to the mean level. But when he wanted something special, or one came to him as it were spontaneously, he could indulge the reader or listener very beautifully. Such passages may occur almost anywhere. A selection of them, some longer, some shorter, some poetical or lyrical and some chiefly of metrical interest, will illustrate his practice. Many more could be submitted. Everyone will have his favorites.

The opening of the General Prologue is one of Chaucer's most studied and carefully composed passages. It is a single longish sentence (128 words) of two balanced parts: *Whan* . . . (eleven lines) and *Than* . . . (seven lines). The first consists of four members: I a (four lines), a formal bipartite structure; I b (two and a half lines); I c (one and a half lines); I d (three lines). Thus I b and I c together, with their four lines, make a kind of balance with I a. The second part consists of two members: II a (three lines) and II b (four lines).

I a. When the sweet showers of April have penetrated (*perced*) the drought of March, i.e., have saturated the dry soil, and have bathed every *veyne* with the moisture which produces flowers. . . . Is this two statements or one? The answer turns on the meaning of *veyne*. If one statement is intended then *veyne* is a variation of *roote*: moisture is absorbed by the roots and rises to make the flowers expand. But it is possible—perhaps less likely—that the

veins are in the leaves, and if so *bathed* is more literal than figurative. The moisture at the roots makes the leaves sprout and the
leaves are in turn sprinkled to encourage the blossoms. The
choice may not seem important, but when recognized it adds
complexity and a kind of richness. There is also the syntax of
swich licour Of which vertu, but this, however parsed, must mean
'that liquid which has the virtue of engendering flowers.'—
The first line is a nine-syllable line, that is, if the now accepted
reading *Aprill* is correct. Chaucer's spelling elsewhere is trisyllabic,
as in *Tr.* 1 156, *Aperil*; and cf. the song 'Bytvene Mersh ant
Averil' (:*wyl*). Manly and Rickert, III, 421, "sought in vain"
for any example with a final -*e*, but they missed the well known
song 'I syng of a mayden,' in which the form is *Aprille*, riming
with *stille* (adv.). *Whan* in the first line is metrically stressed,
though not before *Zephirus*, for there no special emphasis is
needed. A different kind of emphasis results from the position of
droghte, so that *Aprill* and *March* both stand in the second foot—
balance and contrast. And note the chiastic order of *shoures soote*
and *swete breeth*. This emphasis on the first *Whan* contrasts with
the answering *Than*, where a similar emphasis might have been
expected. But the suspense makes up for the absence of metrical
stress. The whole line (12) moreover has its peculiar rhythm.
What with the grammatical inversion, *longen folk* (people now,
not birds), the first three words are rhythmically stressed, and
the last word *pilgrymages* has special emphasis as introducing
the new idea to which all that precedes has been leading up.

1 b. *Whan Zephirus eek.* . . . The *eek* is metrically strengthened
by the inversion of the third foot and points the parallel with
the first two couplets, and also secondarily with the repeated
sweetness: *soote, swete*. The witty use of 'inspire' both literal
and figurative, with a hint of divine afflatus, is the first approach
to the humor which becomes overt in 1 d.

Now 1 c, the shortest of the four, seems to bring the series,
the three aspects of the weather, to a conclusion: April, the
warm wind, the position of the sun, climactically arranged. Manly
notes also a temporal sequence: the April rains have soaked in,

green has begun to show in *holt* and *heeth*, the sun has finished its half-course in passing through the Ram.

But now again in I d attention is drawn to a new aspect, the effect of the spring weather on animate life, the small birds.

I d is of course both the climax of I and a transition to II—the couplet is divided between the two parts. The little birds sing; they are so touched by the vernal spirit that they hardly sleep at night. Nature, the goddess now, so pricks them in their *corages* that they sleep with one eye open, or so Chaucer says, with a smile. Their hearts are strengthened by the return of spring and they feel a new courage to meet the new season. Chaucer does not say, however, that they sing at night. We may at our discretion think of them as nightingales and at the same time wonder if he ever heard nightingales in mid April. The word *priketh* has been sometimes misunderstood. A prick can be painful, though never very painful and certainly not here. Here it is a heartening stimulus—as Nature said to the birds in the Parlement (389): *I prike yow with plesaunce.*

II *Than.* . . . The sentence so built up of its four graduated parts now descends gradually. With all these manifestations of spring people long to be on the road (II a), to go on pilgrimages; everyone becomes a pilgrim, and palmers are added in a parenthesis. And *specially* (II b) from all over England they turn towards Canterbury—a pleasant exaggeration—to the shrine of St. Thomas, who has helped them when they were sick. This last line still needs explanation, but lest it should seem weak Chaucer has given it the appearance of strength by the echo rime with a form for him unique: *seke.*[1]

It has been asked sometimes whether Chaucer intended a difference in meaning or a nuance between *soote* in the first couplet and *swete* in the third. The latter is by all odds Chaucer's usual word. The former occurs eight times in rime and hence may have

---

1. There were two forms of this word in ME, the expected form with $\bar{e}^1$ and another with unexplained *i*. Chaucer has in rime *sik* (adj. sing.) twice and *sike* (adj. plu.) three times. Exceptional is *the syke* (sing.) in *Tr.* II 1572. In the non-Chaucerian parts of RR the form is *sek*, riming with *lek, ek.*

been chosen for this purpose. Elsewhere, i.e., in prose and within a line of verse, it occurs fifteen times, of which thirteen (though the scribes sometimes differ) have it beside a word with a back vowel; hence vowel harmony may have been a determinant. But *swete* is found frequently near words with back vowels; compare also *sweete breeth* A 5 and *swoote breth* LGW F 173, both with *Zepherus*. Chaucer used *swete* for all general purposes, with both persons and things, as a token of approval—unless he needed the other form for rime. For the choice of *soote* in A 1 there might be any one of four reasons, or a combination of them. If the image of rain penetrating to the roots came first, then *soote* was chosen for the rime. Or if *soote* came first as a striking word, most appropriate for the opening line, then the image of *perced to the roote* followed, partly at least for the rime. Third, *soote* may have seemed more euphonious with *shoures* than *swete*. Fourth, Chaucer may have intended, for the passage anyway, some significant difference of meaning. Professor Fisher concluded, after examining all the evidence, that in general *soote* connotes something bland and gentle, *swete* something dear and charming.[2] But in this place the showers of April are more than gentle: they penetrate deep into the soil and turn the dryness of March into the richness of spring. The breath of Zephirus is more than pleasant: it inspires the buds to expand, the flowers to bloom, and the Pilgrims to be on their way.

It should go without saying that throughout this opening paragraph Chaucer is poetic following a long tradition, and is in no sense realistic. We are not to suppose that March was a dry month in the south of England *ca.* 1388; or that the nightingales, if there are any, were English nightingales; or that the *sweete breeth* was a real warm wind blowing across the downs from the Gulf Stream. It was a literary importation, from stock, or perhaps directly from his Boethius: *Zepherus, the debonere wind* [which] *bryngeth ayen in the first somer sesoun the leeves* (Bo i. m. 5). These are all ornaments laid on to warn us that none of this springtime is really real but part of the larger comedy to follow.

2. John H. Fisher, "Chaucer's Use of *Swete* and *Swote*," *JEGP* 50 (1951), 326-31.

Zephirus and the small birds and the Cardinal Archbishop are painted figures opening the way for those special Nine-and-Twenty. The spring gave promise, never quite fulfilled, like many another springtime; and the sweetness can turn to bittersweet. For we recall that Chaucer introduced his two great lovers in *Aperil, whan clothed is the mede With newe grene.*

What follows this set-piece stands out as a fine example of Chaucer writing with a relaxed hand. It appears at first as unduly careless and it certainly is careless in the time sequence. (The pilgrims arrive one day at night and by sunset the narrator has become well acquainted with them all.) Very few of the rime words deserve their important position, e.g., *day : lay.* *Southwerk* is given more prominence than *the Tabard*, which is the real setting. The repetition of *sondry* from the preceding sentence is infelicitous. There are good things, of course, like the repetition of *corage(s) pilgrimyge(s)* in inverse order, and of *wende(n)*, with playful reference to the *corages* of the birds and the narrator's *deuout corage.* This contrast of two styles in two adjacent passages of about equal length is not one of good and bad but of careful workmanship and friendly engaging casualness. Chaucer commanded both styles, and it is only their close juxtaposition here which draws our attention.

Two consecutive stanzas of the *Troilus* (v 239-52) offer a similar contrast between Chaucer at his best and at his second or third best.

> *"How sholde I thus ten dayes ful endure,*
> *Whan I the firste nyght have al this tene?* 240
> *How shal she don ek, sorwful creature?*
> *For tendernesse how shal she ek sustene*
> *Swich wo for me? O pitous, pale, and grene*
> *Shal ben youre fresshe wommanliche face*
> *For longynge, or ye torne into this place."* 245
>
> *And whan he fille in any slomberynges,*
> *Anon bygynne he sholde for to grone,*
> *And dremen of the dredfulleste thynges*

That myghte ben: as mete he were allone
In place horrible, makyng ay his mone,   250
Or meten that he was amonges alle
His enemys, and in hire hondes falle.

The first stanza shows that he could, when he would, write
perfectly. It has all his skill and hardly a flaw. Note the spondees
in almost every line; a slight emphasis on *I* in contrast to *she*,
which though metrically unstressed, acquires emphasis from the
contrast; the postpositive *ek* in 241 and its parallel repetition in
the next line; the varied pauses, first at the line ends, then in the
fifth and seventh within the line; the three questions of two,
one, and one-and-a-half lines. There is only one forced stress—
into.

On the other hand, in the second stanza, *any* looks like padding. There are forced stresses on *for, of, ben, were, was, in*: one
in nearly every line. The second line is thoroughly weak. Are
mete and *meten* both infinitival? The former might be subjunctive. We were moved by the words of Troilus; the poet
made them moving. But his disturbed dreams do not affect us.
The one stanza is composed, the other merely fluent.

There are two v.l. of interest. In 242 γ reads *this* for *ek*.
Robinson has *ek*—eclectically. It can hardly be revision in γ,
since *this* is so much inferior to *ek*. Per contra, in 245 γ has
langour(e) for *longynge*, and since the former is much the
stronger word, it would seem that γ is a revision.

The first stanza of Book II of the *Troilus* is surprising if
not puzzling: Pandarus has taken the love affair in hand; Troilus
is encouraged and feels that first access of Love's ennobling
power. Chaucer now appropriately recalls the opening lines of
the Purgatorio. The image—"la navicella del mio ingegno" and
the boot . . . Of my conning—is the same; and both vessels move
from dark and troubled to brighter waters. But Chaucer has
changed all the rest. He starts with a pure lyric surge:

Owt of thise blake wawes for to saylle,
O wynde, O wynde, the weder gynneth clere.

He does this kind of thing rarely, but never more happily than here; and it is all his own. The infinitival phrase is loosely attached, as though the whole line were an exclamation. The *blake wawes* has built up a tension great enough to compensate and more, for a certain emptiness in the rest of the line. Nevertheless it is an omen. For in the next two lines the separation of *the boot* and its modifier *Of my conning* is awkward and seems to necessitate an emphatic pause after the rime word *travaylle* (the editors insert a comma)—as though the sense were: the boat is in distress. What boat? Why, the boat of my skill. From its position the *I* is a shade too emphatic, and the inversion *it stere* is also awkward. There is no music in the whole line:

Of my ꝁonning that unneth I it steere.

So Chaucer explains: this sea is the tempestuous subject, the despair of Troilus; and now there are signs of hope.

But is this the meaning? Were those black waves the hopelessness of Troilus which the poet had difficulty in describing – he could hardly steer his boat—and is the hope a prospect of smoother sailing in Book II? It doesn't seem so. For he invokes Clio and in the same breath excuses himself as a mere translator. He is an amanuensis of the muse of History. The Book will bring Criseyde to Troilus' bed of feigned sickness, their first meeting in the flesh, and for that he asks to be disblamed. It seems then as though the black waves were in the future. Actually, of course, everything looks both ways. Chaucer had really no difficulty in describing the hero's hopelessness in Book I: the sea was dark for Troilus, not for the poet; the chief difficulty was Pandarus' in getting Troilus to confess; but he will have trouble in bringing the two lovers together. The *tempestous matere* lies ahead, not for Troilus but for the historian (including Pandarus). The hope is for Troilus' success.

Is this all very confusing, or very subtle? Is it possible to say two things at once without overtaxing the audience? Has Chaucer betrayed his dilemma by the loose infinitive, the awkward word order, and the rime-required *matere*? Is there confusion in his mind or only in his verse? or in both? No. The answer is Chaucer's light-hearted view of the matter. The ambiguity is playful. As with a pun, the reader pauses, balances the possibilities, and decides for both together.

At the end of Book III Chaucer substitutes for Troilo's song (*Fil.* III, 74-75) his own, for which he went direct to his translation of Boethius II, m. 8. This new song (apparently not in *a*) is striking first of all for the studied repetition of *that*—twenty-five times in twenty-eight lines (two lines have three)—like a pedal point. Eleven of these are the relative pronoun, varied only once by *which* and that one followed by the filler: *which that* (1751). This filler occurs in three other places: *That that* (1751, 1758) and *if that* (1762). The others introduce noun clauses or express result. Although this device is skilfully managed, it must be conceded that the general meaning is not easy to follow, and editorial punctuation breaks down. Hence the desecration of paraphrase may be justified.

Love, which rules earth and sea and heaven and joins peoples in wholesome alliance and men in virtuous union, binds this accord, [namely]

That the diverse elements of the world are always held harmoniously together; that sun and moon perform their functions—all this Love brings about: [and also]

that the sea is restrained from overflowing the land. And if Love should loosen his bridle, everything which Love now holds together would fall apart.

Therefore, would God that Love be pleased to encircle and bind fast all hearts so that none can escape. And cold hearts, I pray that he turn them to love that they have pity on those who suffer, and that he (Love) preserve those who are true.

(This last is a little puzzling. It would be simpler to read *him* for *hem* in 1770—'that Love would have pity on sore hearts.')

The best commentary however is a comparison of Chaucer's translation of Boethius and his adaptation for the *Troilus*.

He starts with the middle of Boethius' poem:

> *Love, that of erthe and se hath governaunce,* 1744
> *Love, that his hestes hath in hevenes hye, . . .* 1745
> *Bynd this acord.* 1750

al this accordaunce of thynges is bounde with love, that governeth erthe and see, and hath also comandement to the hevene.

Then he skips a few lines of Boethius:

> *Love, that with an holsom alliaunce* 1746
> *Halt peples joyned, as hym list hem gye,*
> *Love, that enditeth lawe of compaignie,*
> *And couples doth in vertu for to dwelle.* 1749

This love halt togidres peples joyned with an holy boond, and knytteth sacrement of mariages of chaste loves; and love enditeth lawes to trewe felawes.

For his second stanza he goes back to Boethius' beginning:

> *That that the world, with feith which that is stable,* 1751
> *Diverseth so his stowndes concordynge,*
> *That elementz that been so discordable*
> *Holden a bond perpetuely durynge.* 1754

That the world with stable feyth varieth accordable chaungynges; that the contrarious qualities of elementz holden among hemself allyaunce perdurable.

> *That Phebus mote his rosy day forth brynge,* 1755
> *And that the mone hath lordshipe over the nyghtes,*
> *Al this doth Love;*

that Phebus, the sonne, with his goldene chariet bryngeth forth the rosene day; that the moone hath commaundement over the nyghtes.

He now passes over Boethius' *whiche nyghtes Esperus, the evesterre, hath brought,* but continues into the third stanza:

> *That that the se, that gredy is to flowen,*   1758
> *Constreyneth to a certeyn ende so*
> *His flodes, that so fiersly they ne growen*
> *To drenchen erthe and al for evere mo:—*   1761

that the see, gredy to flowen, constreyneth with a certein eende his floodes so that it is nat leveful to strecche his brode termes or bowndes uppon the erthes (that is to seyn, to coveren al the erthe).

Now to finish this stanza he skips what he had used for his first lines but picks up Boethius with

> *And if that Love aught lete his bridel go,*   1762
> *Al that now loveth asonder sholde lepe,*
> *And lost were al that Love halt now to hepe.*

And yif this love slakede the bridelis, alle thynges that now loven hem togidres wolden make batayle contynuely, and stryven to fordo the fassoun of this world, the which they now leden in accordable feith by fayre moevynges.

Now for his fourth stanza he has left of Boethius only one closing sentence

> *O weleful were mankynde, yif thilke love that governeth hevene governede yowr corages,*

and this he expands into

> *So wolde God, that auctour is of kynde,*   1765
> *That, with his bond, Love of his vertu liste*
> *To cerclen hertes alle, and faste bynde,*
> *That from his bond no wight the wey out wiste;*

but the stanza still lacks three lines, which Chaucer now fills out by letting Troilus speak—with an amusing change from *wolde God* to *wolde I:*

> *And hertes colde, hem wolde I that he twiste*   1769
> *To make hem love, and that him [hem] liste ay rewe*
> *On hertes sore, and kepe hem that ben trewe.*

It is remarkable how closely he has followed his source, taking over so many words of his translation, and deftly brought into context the heavenly love of Boethius with the earthly love of his poem. The only additions are at the end of the first stanza *that I have told and telle*, made necessary by his having altered the sequence of Boethius; and *ay heried be his myghtes* at the end of the second stanza. Coming where they do they have just the merest air of padding.

There are only three masculine rimes in the twenty-eight, and eleven lines are purely trochaic. The b-rimes of the first stanza (*-ye*)[3] have a kind of echo in the a-rimes of the fourth (*-ynde*). The c-rimes of the first and fourth stanzas have the same vowel (*e*), as do the a- and b-rimes of the third (*o*), with another *o* (*flodes*) inside the line, and likewise the b- and c-rimes of the second (*y*) along with the b-rimes of the fourth (*i*). In the second stanza *concordynge* and *discordable* make an obvious pair. In the fourth the rime word *liste* is echoed by *faste* in the next line and is repeated four lines below. The riming *twiste* makes a strong and surprising figure, occasioned, perhaps induced, by the rime, and rather intensified by the grammatical inversion.

All these details, along with the deliberate repetitions of *that*, make this paean to Love a highly ornate and fitting climax to Book III, when Love has so completely altered the inner spirit of the hero—to say nothing of the covert irony in the closing line: 'guard all true lovers and keep them true who are true.'

Chaucer has a few scattered allusions to music. The nine spheres, he says (PF 61-64), are the well of music and melody in this world, and the cause of harmony; and Troilus, from the eighth sphere, sees the erratic stars and hears the sound of heavenly melody (*Tr.* v 1811-13). On various occasions the birds sing. In his dream in BD the poet heard the *noyse and swetnesse*

3. For the β reading *enditeth* (1748) as in Root, γ has *knetteth*, making a nine-syllable line. Both words are in Boethius (both are in Chaucer's translation and match *dictat* and *nectit* of the Latin), so that it is impossible to say, from this passage, which is original and which is revision; but one notes that the *i* of *enditeth* repeats the b-rimes of the stanza.

of their song, like a solemn service, an almost celestial harmony, as some sang low, some high. In the Garden of Love (PF 191) they sang with angelic voices. In the Hall of Fame he heard

> *the hevenyssh melodye*
> *Of songes, ful of armonye.*   HF 1395-96

In the Parlement he heard the ravishing sweetness of stringed instruments—God himself never heard better, *as I gesse* (PF 197-200). Sarpedon entertained Troilus with instrumental music—woodwinds and strings—but it made him melancholy because Criseyde was not there. At the court of Cambyuskan there was heavenly music of various instruments (F 270). And so on. But the language is always conventional and there is nothing to show that Chaucer had a musical *ear* any better than Charles Lamb's. That he enjoyed listening to music there is nothing to tell us or that he appreciated music musically. Yet he certainly had an ear for verbal music and he might have talked pleasantly, on even terms, with two of our most musical poets, Tennyson and Swinburne, who were both indifferent to music as music.

Chaucer's verbal music breaks out in many, even in unlikely, places. It is not unexpected in

> *And clepe ayeyn the beaute of youre face*   Tr. v 914
> *The fresshe beaute sleeth me sodenyly*
> *Of hire that rometh in the yonder place;*   A 1118-19

(which is a little damaged when we recall

> *Your yen two wol slee me sodenly*

of the Merciles Beaute balades, with their humorous ending); and it is laid-on beauty in

> *The bisy larke messager of day*
> *Salueth in hir song the morwe gray*
> *And firy Phebus riseth vp so brighte*
> *That al the orient laugheth of the lighte*
> *And with his stremes dryeth in the greues*
> *The siluer dropes hangyne on the leues.*   A 1491-96

But surely we were not prepared for it in

> *There spryngen herbes grete and smale*
> *The licorys and the cetewale*
> *   And many a clowe gylofre*
> *And notemuge to put in ale*
> *Wheither it be moyste or stale*
> *   Or for to leye in cofre*
>
> *The briddes synge it is no nay*
> *The sparhauk and the popyniay*
> *   That ioye it was to here*
> *The thrustelcock made eek his lay*
> *The wodedowue up on the spray*
> *   She sang ful loude and clere.*   B 1950-61

The burlesque is very lightly touched in: stale ale and the singing of hawk and parrot. (Manly comments, with rare editorial felicity: "The sweet notes of the sparrow hawk and the parrot well offset the loud, clear voice of the wooddove.") We may stumble over *gilófre*, and *notemuge* does not look quite right; but the illusion is all there, and the implied music; and we are pleased to remember too that these herbs came originally from the rose garden of Guillaume de Loris, and that two of them sweetened the room of Hende Nicholas (A 3207). Thus we enjoy the little surprise. Doggerel? Another of the poet's little gibes at the Host.

There is another surprise in the Invocation to the mysterious piece about Feire Anelida and Fals Arcite—

> *Be favorable eke, thou Polymya,*
> *On Parnaso that with thy sustres glade*
> *By Elycon, not fer from Cirrea,*
> *Singest with vois memorial in the shade*
> *Under the laurer which that may not fade*

—a Miltonic marshaling of high-sounding names, a sustained melody of repeated *a* sounds, and the sudden *memorial*, a blend of memorable, immemorial, and that extra something which is the magic.

Then there is Arcite's little song, A 1510-12—it is hardly more than a token—and nicely fitted into the narrative couplets. Two of the three lines are headless, with proper emphasis on the first syllable. The first line begins with *May*, the second ends with *May*, and the third ends with *may* (an echo rime). One notes the *f* and *g* alliteration. The song is really a pointed plea. Arcite has ridden a mile or two from the palace meditating on *the poynt of his desir*. He dismounts in a grove to make himself a garland, and sings: May the fresh green of May bring me *som grene*— which turns to irony, for his *grene* is found to be as transient as that of May itself.

Rosemounde is a pleasant example of Chaucer's skilful blend of lyric and humour. There are three uncertain lines.

Madame, ye ben of al beaute shryne

has tempted some editors to read *alle,* without authority in Chaucer's usage; Globe inserts [*the*]; otherwise the rhythm is peculiar, even if *Madame* is taken as three syllables. In l. 4 *lyke ruby* (Skeat, Globe, Robinson) may be a scribal error for *lyk a*; elsewhere *lyk* in this sense is always a monosyllable. Again, in l. 6 the second *that* is metrically superfluous and probably also a scribal error.

Of the six a-rimes two are of French origin: *galantyne* and *devyne*; and both *tyne* and *out-twyne* (if a compound) are Chaucerian hapaxes; *twine* alone occurs in *Tr.* v 7. Of the twelve b-rimes eight are French; and *mapemounde* and *afounde* are hapaxes. All four of the c-rimes are French. There are near-echo rimes in *confounde founde affounde*, and in *mapemounde Rosemounde*. These rimes, while they do not point to a French source, do suggest a Gallic attitude.

The lady's *smal* voice reminds us inevitably of the Pardoner's (A 688, like a goat's) and of Absolon's (A 3360, *gentil and smal*); it was thin and high pitched, perhaps whining. In the fourth line there is a possible ambiguity intended: your round cheeks are like a ruby, *or* your cheeks are like round rubies, i.e., have bright red spots. Towards the end there is a playful mixture of imagery:

ve burns so hot that it cannot be either chilled in the ordi-
way or quenched in water.

nother piece of wit and clever riming is the Triple Roundel
of Merciles Beaute, which though still regarded as 'doubtful' must
certainly be Chaucer's—unless we have lost an equally good
poet.

The first roundel begins easily, with easy rimes in -*ly* and with
the five rimes in -*ene*—a grave lover's complaint, albeit in conventional language. In the second roundel the three a-rimes are a bit
unusual, with the echo of *chaced purchaced*; and the five b-rimes
resemble but do not exactly match the b-rimes of the first (-*eyne*
and -*ene*) and the gravity is only slightly relaxed by *me nedeth
not to feyne*. Then in the third all the cards are down. The a-
rimes shift from -*aced* to the blunt -*at* and lead off with the un-
poetic word *fat*; the b-rimes actually repeat the b-rimes of the
first roundel (with echo rimes of *mene* [v.b.] and *mene* [n.]) except that the latter are $\bar{e}^1$ and the new ones are $\bar{e}^2$: ten different
words in -*ene*.

One of Chaucer's finest displays of purple is given to the
Wife of Bath—one of the little surprises of her Tale. In those
first twenty-five lines, which are themselves a perfect introduction to her story, there is a rich blend of nostalgic charm
and contemporary satire; and the passage is sanctified for modern
readers by the line

> *As thikke as motes in the sonne beem,*   D 868

which Milton—"celestial thief," Swinburne called him—appro-
priated.

Structurally the passage is made up of six groups: the opening triad, then two lines, then two lines which are not a couplet,
then nine lines ending with a couplet; six lines of slur direct
against the Friar (whose Tale is to follow; note *lymytour* in 874
and in 1265), and three lines to finish off the satire. As the fourth
group (864-72) ends with a unit line—

> *This maketh that ther been no fairyes——*   D 872

which pulls the sentence together, so the next group ends with a unit line which points up the satire and closes the couplet—

> *Wommen may go saufly up and doun.*   D 878

As the fourth group emphasizes *Now* (864) and *Now* (865), so the next echoes it *now* (874). In Manly's cd* group of manuscripts and a few others an additional *now* is inserted (so Globe and Robinson, but not Skeat), but the line is a good nine-syllable one without it, bringing emphasis on the first word *Wommen*, where it belongs.

Besides the remarkable run of three all-trochaic lines (see p. 97) there are a few other metrical details to note.

> *For now the grete charitee and prayeres*   D 865

will scan only by either reducing *charitee* to a disyllable or by violent elision (*-tee and*). The accentuation of *prayéres* is certain: it occurs five times besides here, always with *freres* (A 231, D 1884, 1905, 1911, 1939).

> *As he gooth in his lymytacioun*   D 877

is also peculiar, putting all the weight of the line on one word: literally the limits of his allotted district (as also in Wiclif), but here with a twist for his business of being a limitour. The last line has troubled commentators:

> *And he ne wol doon hem but dishonour.*

The literal-minded, including a goodly number of scribes stemmatically related and unrelated, read *no* for *but*, as well as Globe and Koch; but they miss the meaning of the Wife's final flaunt. Robinson nails it down firmly: "The friar brought only dishonor upon a woman; the incubus always caused conception."

The touches of *fairye*, so appropriate to give the pitch for what follows, need no pointing. They are echoed later when the knight meets four and twenty ladies dancing *vnder a forest syde* (989-92). The *o* sounds of

> *But now kan no man se none elues mo*   D 864

are a distinct embellishment; and so is the weighted word *serchen*

7): these limitors go prowling everywhere with their pre-
:e of *Blessynge*. . . .

Along with the Wife's delicate language here, in contrast to
the forthrightness of her language throughout her Prologue,
Chaucer has added a flicker of his own ambivalent humor:

> *This was the olde opynyoun as I rede.*   D 862

The Wife's reading was presumably confined to hearing her
Fifth Husband read from his cursed books.

The Old Hag in WBT lectures her young knight on the
charges (which he has not really made against her) that she is
ugly, old, and poor. To this third charge she devotes thirty lines
beginning

> *And ther as ye of pouerte me repreue*   D 1177

and ending

> *Of my pouerte namoore ye me repreue.*   D 1206

Midway she says

> *Verray pouerte it singeth proprely.*   D 1191

The word *singeth* is the reading of all the editors except Manly,
who nevertheless regards it as correct. It is also an echo of Juv-
enal's line (x, 22) "cantabit vacuus coram latrone viator," which
Chaucer at once translates (and which he used in the gloss at
the end of Boece II, p. 5). Here Chaucer enforces the singing by
conspicuously repeating *pouerte* eleven times—like the pedal point
on *that*, in *Tr.* III 1744-71.[4]

Somewhat similarly Chaucer plays on the *o* and *u* sounds in
six lines (A 3981-86) describing the plans of the Trumpington
parson for marrying his daughter: *bistowe, blood, holy, good
moot, holy, blood, wolde, holy blood, holy, sholde*; and *worthy,
honoure, deuoure.* An equally striking example is in Theseus'
humorous commentary on Palamon's and Arcite's love for Emily:

4. Famous examples of this are the fugue in the third movement of
the Brahms *Requiem*, and Chopin's so-called Raindrop Prelude, op. 28, no.
15.

woot namoore, hoote, woot, moot, hoot and coold, moot, fool, cold, woot, yore agoon, oon, knowe, woot, sore in eight lines (A 1809-16); and another, *anon oon, anon, oother, agon* (A 2334-36); and still another with a surprise ending:

> *O persone allone with outen mo*
> *And haryed forth by arm foot and too.* A 2725-26

Such things can hardly be accidental. Rather different is

> *and wo was hym to gon to sone;*
> *But torne he mooste, and it was ek to done,* Tr. v 69-70

and just after the Cantus the rimes *soone olde doone byholde tolde* (v 645-49) with *moone* in 648 and 649; followed after one intervening stanza by *tho do mo* (660/62/63), then *so soote boote* (671/72) and *moore soore* (673/75).

At the beginning of the Wife's Tale Chaucer has a very unusual display of three consecutive trochaic lines, thus reversing the prevailing iambic movement, with thirteen words in a row which are each a trochee:

> *Blessynge halles chambres kichenes boures*
> *Citees burghes castels hye toures*
> *Thropes bernes shipnes dayeryes.* D 869-71

This can be no accident. But it is nothing beside the *bravura* of D 655-58 in the Wife's Prologue, where he took a proverbial jingle of rough four-stress verses—

> *Who that byldeth his howse all of salos,*
> *And prikketh a blynde horsse over the falowes,*
> *And suffereth his wif to seke many halos,*
> *God send hym the blisse of everlasting galos!*

and made them over, with a minimum of change, to fit easily into his staple five-stress lines:

> *Who so that buyldeth his hous al of salwes*
> *And priketh his blynde hors ouer the falwes*
> *And suffreth his wyf to go seken halwes*
> *Is worthy to be hanged on the galwes.* D 655-58

The Night Spell in MillT makes a good offset to this:

Iesu Crist and seint Benedight
Blesse this hous from euery wikked wight
For the nyghtes uerye the white Pater noster
Where wentestow seint Petres soster.　　A 3483-86

Manly notes (III, 441): "Until this charm is better understood we cannot be sure of several words, as the scribes were obviously puzzled." Robinson in the course of a long note (p. 685) says that the meter is "rough." But the first and last lines are plainly four-stress, like those in the example above, and it is equally plain that Chaucer did not try, as he did in the Wife's Prologue, to accommodate them to the surrounding couplets.

Lenuoy de Chaucer, E 1177-1212, is a show piece of the first water, regardless of who recites it; a riming exhibit of six stanzas on three rimes, *ababcb*—twelve of a, eighteen of b, and six of c holding the group together. The c-rimes are ordinary. The a-rimes in *-ence* are all natural. But the series of b-rimes could not have come without effort. They begin with *Ytaille* which harks far back to *Ytaille vitaille* of the first stanza. They are all of romance origin except *nayle*.

The lines themselves are normal: nine with a weak fourth foot, three with a weak second, two with a weak third, but only one with a weak first foot.

There are genuine spondees in

In jalousie I rede eek thow hym bynde,　　1205
To gete thee freendes ay do thy travaille,　　1210

and rather special is

Beth egre as a tigre yond in Ynde,　　1199

which calls for hiatus *egre as*, evidently for the quasi-rime. (The hiatus of *The arwes* 1203 is arbitrary.) One line starts with two trochees: *Folweth Ekko* 1189. The fourfold alliteration on *l* in the last two lines and the three *w*'s in the last make a sort of climax, to say nothing of the lilt of *as light as leef on lynde*.

In 1197 *men* is almost a pun: in the sense first of 'one,' and then of males. There may be another pun in *couche* 1206: Bind a man with jealousy and you will make him lie down in bed for your pleasure; also, after a dramatic pause, not only submit, but crouch, cower, quail—like a quail. The primary meanings of bed or couch, and as verb to place, are attested in D 88 etc., A 3211, G 1152, etc. The other sense, of crouch or cower, is found only here.

But these prosodic details are only a small part of the extraordinary *vivace* sarcasm of the whole.

In Anelida's Compleynt (*ca.* 1380?) Chaucer has left us a veritable studio-piece of *art poetical* and *maistrye*. The emphasis is on metrical structure and riming, for the lines themselves are unusually smooth and regular.[5] Only two might make a reader hesitate:

> *Your sovereyne lady in this world here*   252
> *Of my dedly adversite.*   258

The opening and concluding image (from Dante) is part of the *bravura*:

> *So thirleth with the poynt of remembraunce*   ｜4529ᴕ
> *The swerd of sorrow, . . .*   211-12
>   *. . . so sore*
> *Hath thirled with the poynt of remembraunce;*   349-50

and *the swerd of sorrow* is repeated 270. There is one striking figure in

> *Your chere floureth, but it wol not sede*   306

(*sede* is a Chaucerian hapax); and another in

> *As in a tempest is a roten mast.*   314

The Compleynt comprises 141 lines (Anel 211-350) and consists of two parts, Part I and Part II, which are metrically identical, enclosed in a frame of an introductory (211-19) and a con-

5. Robinson's text is especially eclectic for this poem, but none of the peculiar manuscript variants seriously affects the following analysis. The terms *strophe* and *antistrophe* employed by the editors are misleading, inasmuch as they suggest the Greek choral odes.

cluding stanza (342-50) riming $aabaabbab^5$—which is the basic stanzaic pattern throughout. Part I and its matching Part II are made up as follows: A. four stanzas (1, 2, 3, 4) of the basic pattern $aabaabbab^5$ (220-55); B. one stanza of 16 lines (256-71) aaa^4 $b^5aaa^4b^5$ and this scheme reversed, $bbb^4a^5bbb^4a^5$ (that is, the a lines of the basic pattern are shortened to four stresses and increased from two to three, and then continued with the rimes reversed); and finally C. which returns to the basic pattern but, for a triumphant climax, has two internal rimes in each of its nine lines, $a^{cc}a^{dd}b^{ee}a^{ff}a^{gg}b^{hh}b^{ii}a^{jj}b^{kk}$. Then all this is repeated: II A (281-316), B (317-32), C (333-41).

Along with this highly organized complexity of structure there are elaborate weavings and repetitions of the riming sounds. To mark the enclosing frame, the a-rimes of the introductory stanza are the b-rimes of the concluding stanza. The b-rimes of the introductory stanza recur as the b-rimes of the first stanza of II.A. The a-rimes of the concluding stanza have been anticipated by the b-rimes of I.A.3.

Further, the a-rimes of I.A.1 reappear as the internal rimes of II.C. line 1. The b-rimes of I.A.2 (*-eyne*) match the a-rimes of II.A.1 and resemble the a-rimes (*-eyn*) of II.A.4. The a-rimes of I.A.4 (*-esse*) are repeated in the b-rimes of II.A.2. The a-rimes of I.B recur as internal rimes in the next stanza, I.C, lines 2 and 5. The internal rimes of this same stanza, line 3, recur as the b-rimes of the next stanza, II.A.1. But the supreme exhibit is II.A.3 (299-307), where the five a-rimes are in-*ẹde* and the four b-rimes in *-ẹde,* the open and close *e's* carefully distinguished; and two of these recur as internal rimes in II.C, line 8.

There are several echo rimes: *preye* (1st pers. sing.) *preye* (infin.) 318/32; *asure asure* 330/31; *drye drie* 333/36; *more evermore* 240/46, 342/43; *stidfast fast* 310/13; *-les* 229/30/36 *les* 233; and so far apart as hardly to count *trewe* 216 *untrewe* within 274.

Altogether there are 141 end rimes and 36 internal rimes, or 177 riming words. Of these words comparatively few are repeated; *me* three times (two of them internal); *ye, be, adversite, day, drede* twice each (one in each case internal); *more, evermore* twice each; *remembraunce, peyne, pleyne, hevynesse* once each;

and also *hewe, trewe, rewe, newe,* which are the b-rimes of the introductory stanza and the b-rimes of II.A.1. The five a-rimes of I.A.4 and the four b-rimes of II.A.2 are in *-esse,* but only *hevynesse,* is repeated. The five a-rimes of the introductory stanza and the four b-rimes of the concluding stanza are in *-aunce,* but only one word, *remembraunce,* is repeated.

All these various details testify to the magnitude of Chaucer's *tour de force,* to say nothing of the special stanza of nine rimes in *-ede* (five $\bar{e}^1$, four $\bar{e}^2$). The astonishing thing is that Chaucer should have indulged his muse in such a display of 'transcendent execution.' It is as though he was responding to some challenge, to show himself (or someone else?) what he could do when he wanted to. And he crowns the miracle by making sense, if not poetry, of the words. There are many examples of fancy riming in Froissart, Machaut, and Deschamps, and many examples of internal rime in mediaeval Latin verse, but nothing which can be regarded as a model of Anelida's Compleynt has ever been found. There was nothing like it before;[6] one would be hard pressed to find anything like it since.[7]

The Parlement of Foules has been a mare's nest for those commentators who, to the neglect of its paramount humor, seek earnestly for profound meanings in it. Its structural organization may leave something to be desired; but as one of Chaucer's otherwise most carefully written poems, with unfailing grace and lightness, it merits a place among our collection of displays of *art poetical* and *maistrye.* In ease and smoothness it equals and prob-

6. His own so-called Complaint of Venus, a triple balade with one envoy, taken from Graunson, is another example of riming craftily. Each of the three balades has three stanzas *ababbccb,* each with its own rimes, except that the a-rimes (*-aunce*) of the first recur as the c-rimes of the second and also as the four b-rimes of the envoy, thus making a sort of frame or return. The words *suffisaunce remembraunce* of the first balade and *plesaunce* of the second balade are repeated in the envoy.

7. Dunbar's 'Ane Ballat of our Lady' ("Hale sterne, superne! Hale, in eterne") consists of seven stanzas $a^4b^3a^4b^3a^4b^3a^4b^3—b^3a^4b^3$ (with *Ave Maria, gracia plena* after the eighth line), all five a-lines having two internal rimes on the same sound; i.e., fifteen a-rimes and six b-rimes in each stanza, and nearly all the b-lines contain alliteration.

ably surpasses anything he ever did, as well as in its varied mingling of lyric and narrative, of descriptive and conversational passages. It is purple all through.

Compare first the opening and concluding lines. One does
not miss the shortness and sharpness in the metrical parallelism of

> *The lyf so short . . .*
> *Th'assay so hard . . .*

Then the variation in *the craft so* and *so sharp the* avoids any
woodenness. The third line repeats the pause after the fourth syllable, then the pattern is varied by putting the verb before *so
yerne*. After this brisk beginning the stanza is loosened: the movement changes to

> *Al this mene I by Love*
> *that my felynge Astonyeth,*

drops almost to prose,

> *with his wonderful werkynge,*

and then returns to the 2 + 3 pattern:

> *So sore, iwis,*
> *that whan I on hym thinke,*
> *Nat wot I wel*
> *wher that I flete or synke—*

with alliteration (*iwis, I wel*) but without the former abrupt-
ness.

The artistic climax of the poem is of course the rondel; but
a final stanza was necessary to finish the 'story,' to rouse the
dreamer and assure us that his dream was all a disappointment.
The stanza is prosodically rather routine, but one notes the three
lines with pause after the first foot—*I wok . . . , I hope . . . , The
bet . . .* , and the *o* sounds for playful emphasis in

> *I wok, and othere bokes toke me to.*

In *I hope, ywis* there is an echo of *So sore iwis* in the first stanza.

The number of really irregular lines is remarkably small, some
of them a matter of scribal or editorial vagary. Note

> *Th'eschewing is only the remedye* 140

(with inversion in the third foot, perhaps for emphasis);

> *That hot, cold, hevy, lyght, moyst, and dreye* 380

(which Robinson accepts as a possible Lydgate line; other editors insert *and* before *moyst*);

> *Than som man doth that hath served ful yore* 476

(an awkward line; no v. l. recorded; probably to be read with inversion in both third and fourth feet: *thát hath sérved*);

> *And whoso hit doth, ful foule hymself acloyeth* 517

(*hit* is in GgCx only; Globe and Skeat omit it. Possibly elision -*so hit*, or a trisyllabic foot. The *And* could be spared);

> *Of knyghthod, and lengest had used it* 549

(which could be easily smoothed by reading *had lengest*).

On the other hand, there is a goodly number of facultative anapests (avoidable only by improbable contractions and elisions), in harmony with the poem's lightness. For example

> | | |
> |---|---|
> | *Chapitres sevene it hadde, of hevene and helle* | 32 |
> | *That nevere was ther grevaunce of hot ne cold* | 205 |
> | *Foolhardynesse, Flaterye, and Desyr* | 227 |
> | *Biblis, Dido, Thisbe, and Piramus* | 289 |
> | *The gentyl faucoun, that with his feet distreyneth* | 337 |
> | *And syn that non loveth hir so wel as I* | 435 |
> | *Or at the leste I love hire as wel as ye* | 452 |
> | *And lenger have served hire in my degre* | 453 |
> | *Unkynde, janglere, or rebel any wyse* | 457 |
> | *But I dar seyn, I am hire treweste man* | 479 |
> | *And herkeneth which a resoun I shal forth bringe* | 564 |
> | *That she hireself shal han hir eleccioun* | 621 |
> | *Thankynge alwey the noble goddesse of kynde.* | 672 |

The rhythm of three lines deserves particular praise:

> *Forth with his make, ór with his lady deere* 466

(emphasis on *or*);

> *For to delyvere us is grét charite* 508

(emphasis on *gret*);

> *Lyve thow soleyn, wormes corupcioun*   614

(heavy sarcasm and contempt).

Of the seven nine-syllable lines only two (445, 641) begin with a weak syllable.

There are two run-on stanzas (154, 155 and 343, 344 in the list of birds) and a third which is quite remarkable:

> *And ferther in the temple I gan espie*   280
>
> *That, in dispit . . .*   281

Alliteration is plentiful but not especially noteworthy unless where it is threefold, as in 46-47, 192, 299, 680. But the tree stanza (176-82), already mentioned for its pauses, is loaded with alliteration: *byldere box-, ok ek asshe elm ew asp eke, piler pipere playne pleyne pes palm, cofre careyne, lashe olyve laurer, saylynge cipresse, vyne victor devyne.*

The rimes have several points of interest. Chaucer plays one of his favorites in

> *place grace* 43/45, 83/84, 127/29, 412/13, 421/23
> *face place* 155/57
> *place solace* 295/97
> *space place* 314/15
> *place space trace* 51/53/54
> *grace space place* 65/67/68
> *face grace place* 317/19/20——

twenty-five rimes in *-ace*, some of them in close proximity and nearly all in the first half of the poem; the word *grace* seven times, *place* eleven times. The rimes in *-ere* are both well spaced and diverse: fifteen different words (including *here* in its two meanings), eight of which are not repeated; *yere, were* used four times each, and *here* (in its two meanings) six times—

> *yere lere matere* 23/25/26
> *deere apere* 41/42
> *deere cleere* 76/77
> *were there* 106/08

spere bere were 135/37/38
were fere 141/43
weere there yeere 233/35/36
yeere theere 321/22
heere feere yeere 408/10/11
cheere fere 414/16
heere deere heere 464/66/67
manere here 533/35
heere here 657/58.

There are several rimes in *-ed(e)*, some rather curious: *dede* occurs twice (8, 82) in the sense of act, fact, and twice (79, 187) meaning dead, but once *ded* (585) with the same meaning; *rede* the color (186) and *red* the color (583).

There is a large proportion of echo rimes, one of them *heere* twice (464/67, 657/58), others at lines 79/82, 181/82, 310/12, 358/60, 583/86, 608/09, 653/56, 667/69.

The pair *blysse mysse* is repeated 39/40, 72/75. Other obvious repetitions are *I gesse* 160, 200, 223; *grene* 296, 328; *ravyne* 323, 336. Rimes in *-ye, -ie* are common, and in *-e*, the latter beginning with *quantite he thre* 58/60/61, and noticeable for their proximity are *me the be* 156/58/59 and in the next stanza *se be he* 163/65/66. There is similar linking of stanzas when the c-rimes of the second stanza, *sore moore*, become the a-rimes of the third, *lore yoore*; the b-rimes *spere bere were* 135/37/38 are the a-rimes of the following stanza, *were fere*, 141/43; the c-rimes in *-ure* 300/01 are the b-rimes of the following stanza 303/05/06, with *mesure* repeated; so again 314/15, 317/19/20; 358/60, 365/67; 408/10/11, 414/16; and 526/28, 534/36/37. Almost the same are *bone sone* 643/44, *anon gon* 645/47. Towards the end of the poem two consecutive stanzas have the same c-rimes 671/72, 678/79. In the very first stanza the b-rimes in *-ynge* are echoed by the c-rimes *thynke synke*; so later the b-rimes *weere there yeere* 233/35/36 resemble the following c-rimes *payre peyre*; and the b-rimes *hond fond sond* 240/42/43 are like those of the second next stanza, *stonde honde fonde*, 254/56/57; the b-rimes 611/13/14 and 618/20/21 are all six in *-oun* and all with different words.

It goes without saying that all these repetitions, echoes, and interweavings contribute markedly to the lyrical mood and effect of the poem.

Looked at from the outside the Parlement has its place, in the larger French tradition, with Chaucer's other Love Visions, each very different from the other. The Book of the Duchess is the closest to type yet combines praise of the Duke as courtly lover with an elegy for his Duchess. The House of Fame is farthest from typical; it seems at first to be about love (the Dido and Aeneas story, the poet's ignorance of love), but turns to a discussion of Rumor-and-Fame, and stops without the conclusion which might conceivably have forged the whole into a kind of unity. But the Parlement is concerned with Love throughout; it is dedicated, so to say, to Venus. The long introduction is characteristic of Chaucer: the mention of St. Valentine comes only at line 309, almost half way; and until this there has been no sign—except the title—that the poem will be about birds. Then just past the middle come the *poynt*, the formal wooing of the three Eagles, which misled so many early scholars to seek a key in contemporary court circles. This wooing is of course a focal point. The suitors, while they occupy only ten stanzas, argue till nightfall, and their pleas are so unimpressive that the decision is taken over by the feathered M. P.'s and everybody loses patience. The consequent wrangling gets so out of hand that the Speaker— who is no other than Nature, a goddess and God's Vicar—calls them to order; and the Tercel emphasizes the futility by declining any suitor for a year. The lesser birds are, however, awarded their mates; they burst happily into song (with a French tune); and their noise wakens the dreamer. He sighs and reaches for another book, hoping for better success next time. All this is what came of reading Cicero and Macrobius; it was not, he says, what he wanted.

Looked at from within, the poem is a lighthearted travesty on parliamentary procedure. The question under debate is love, and love, the biological urge, is not a subject for argument. But this makes up so little of the poem. It is only the framework, and patently it is not a framework for any profound solution of human problems. African offers six stanzas of admirable wisdom (the one wholly serious passage), but this is out of the book over which the poet fell asleep, and no more is heard of it. For the rest, everything is lightness and brightness, from the poet's pretended astonishment at the wonderful workings of love in the first stanza to the pretended repudiation of his dream in the last stanza. The humor ranges from the dull speeches of the Eagles to the low comedy of the other birds, from the mock invocation to Venus, observed NNW, to the shy denial of the Tercel. The mild satire points so many directions that one would not care to say what exactly was the target; probably there was none. The grave African ushers the dreamer into the Garden of Love, peopled with naked Beauty, Venus almost the same, Priapus, and all their company, and then reminds him that here is something to write about. And withal the writing manifests such zest and charm, such richness of allusion—so thoroughly explored by Dr. Bennett—such profusion of lovely detail, with catalogues of birds and trees and lovers, so many lyrical and descriptive passages, such wealth of gaiety, that the critics seem to have lost their way in its manifold variety.

On this comedy of manners, with birds as persons and enough hints to tempt those who might look for local actors, Chaucer has lavished, as nowhere else, all his art of poetry. It is his nearest approach to pure art, conceived and composed *dans un jet* with the best technical dexterity in his power: happy phrasing and easy fluency, subtleties of versifying and interweaving of rimes, always appropriate to the different wide-ranging kinds of humorous expression, now delicate, now rough, now casual seeming, now deliberately contrived. If ever Beauty is Truth, here it is; and it is enough.

THE rhythm of Chaucer's verse is a composite of the rhythm of contemporary spoken prose and the metrical forms which he adopted. Of these two components the first is for us almost entirely a matter of inference. We assume a knowledge of the individual vowel and consonant sounds, but of the structural patterns of his spoken language—intonation, pitch, tempo, and so on—we know very little. We can gather something from his use of colloquial language fitted to his metrical forms and from a comparison of his verse with the prose of his translations, itself colored by the French and Latin (both for us silent languages) which lay before him. His metrical forms are themselves a matter of inference, based partly on his native English models and on the models which he adapted from across the Channel, and partly also on what we can trace in later developments, so far as they can be attributed to Chaucer's influence. (Lydgate is here a notorious stumblingblock.) Some portion of his audience, the Court primarily, who were acquainted with French poetry, were able to appreciate, as we are not, his modulations of French verse into English and could recognize the differences between their normal usage and his poetical style. His ear must have taken into account the grouping of accented and unaccented syllables in a pleasing order, with a fairly regular alternation, but varied to avoid monotony and with necessary concession to rhetorical or prose emphasis. This is what Saintsbury meant by "his instinctive genius for prosody."

Because of these uncertainties it seemed best to begin—after a sketch of the background of theory—with an attempt to establish Chaucer's practice in handling his favorite five-stress line, and then his four-stress line. The conclusions justified by a deductive examination of the 'facts' are that Chaucer's ear was adjusted to a series of five (or four) iambs to the line of verse and that whether he counted syllables or not the average works out at ten (or eight) syllables to the line. It is usually possible to reduce or expand each line to a theoretical number of syllables by recourse to elision, syncope, etc., and hiatus, imported from Romance versification; but it does not follow that Chaucer read his lines so or meant them to be read so. Rather, it would follow that since he employed all the allowable devices of inversion and substitution (less than full stress in the stressed position and more than light stress in the unstressed position) which are familiar to us in modern verse, he admitted in the interest of variety and for special effect occasional extra syllables regardless of possible elision, syncope, etc. Further he would, when he chose for whatever reasons, including perhaps impatience or indifference, wrench the iambic pattern almost beyond easy recognition; and this last he was more inclined to do in the four-stress line, owing probably to the roughness of this line in the English romances and other poems with which he was familiar.

In his choice of rimes Chaucer allowed himself a similar freedom. In grouping the lines he favored the couplet and next to that the seven-line rime royal stanza, both no doubt as most 'suitable' for narrative. But he adopted from his French models other stanzaic patterns for particular purposes.

So much for the mechanics of his versification. Examples have been submitted freely to illustrate the smooth and the rough and their multiple variations. Because it represents a somewhat peculiar treatment of the line, the Canon's Yeoman's Prologue and Tale has been examined in some detail, in Appendix 2.

Chapter II, on prosody as distinguished from meter, is the more important part of our study. For prosody includes not just the formal or technical aspects of versification, but the *extra* enrichments of language which accompany the use of metrical forms. These may verge sometimes towards rhetoric and style itself, but they belong in such a study because they are regular characteristics of verse and are found only incidentally in prose. The words of a poet have meaning in themselves and increased meaning in their special combinations. It is the same with their sounds. And by the way in which both are put together each influences the other, for better, for worse; so that the sound is inte-

grated in the meaning. Hence the neglect of the one is a diminu-
tion of the other, for both poet and reader.[1]

Here one must first report the obvious and familiar: his
crisp handling of the line as line and his freedom in grouping
the lines, in moulding the couplet or the stanza to match the
natural flow of his sentences; occasionaly also the sacrifice of syntax to the requirements of meter. Beyond this there is danger of
seeing 'beauties' because one is looking for them, the risk of mis-
taking fortuitous felicities for conscious artistry. Chaucer would
subscribe to Keats' surprising dictum: "if poetry comes not as
naturally as the leaves to a tree it had better not come at all"—
understanding prosodic effect for "poetry." He would have understood William Morris' view that one should be able to compose
poetry while weaving tapestry.

Naturalness is the key. Chaucer's verse is eminently natural.
He rarely seems anxious about the next word or the next rime;
it comes right or else a ready substitute will serve. A little padding
or a little dodge and the obstacle is avoided; the verse flows on.
The cult of perfection, the laborious orient ivory, the carving
of cherry-stones is not his way. Even a small gift of humor teaches
that perfection is deceptive, a waste of effort. Verse itself is
artificial; to insist on scrupulous expertise everywhere is to
thwart the illusion of speaking narrative, to intrude needless
blockage between story teller and listener. He knew his audience.
Only once did he descend to ingenuity and let form dominate
completely over matter, as though Anelida could assuage her
hurt heart with metrical *brio*.

Miss Everett, at the beginning of her reflections on Chaucer's
art poetical and *craft* (HF 1095, 1100)[2] assumes, and of course
rightly, that these phrases imply "knowledge of how to write

1. "The order of words and sounds *ought* to induce the proper reading"
(Ezra Pound). When the order is right, syntactically and metrically, the
poetry is quickened; but any imperfection in that order interferes not only
with the proper reading but also with a successful communication. The
medal has two sides.

2. Dorothy Everett, "Some Reflections on Chaucer's 'art poetical,'" a
British Academy lecture (1950) reprinted in *Essays on Middle English
Literature*, Oxford, 1955, pp. 149-74.

poetry (or skill in writing it) according to established rules";
and she adds on the next page that "they suggest a conscious-
ness on his part" of "poetic art (or, as we might call it, technique)." This technique, however, is mainly one of methods of
presentation and organization. The rhetoricians from whom
Chaucer learned some of them had nothing to tell him about the
art of writing verse as verse. It remains then a question whether
he was acutely conscious of the principles of versification in the
narrower sense. No poet, to be sure, composes in metrical language without some awareness of these principles, but how much
thought and care Chaucer gave to them we can but guess. In
another place,[3] Miss Everett admits: "It is possible that his easy
mastery of a variety of metres and styles is in part due to"
his Good Ear. It was the same with Yeats: he was not interested
in metrical theory but he could ring all the changes without it.

For the most part, in truth, Chaucer's versification is skilful
rather than masterly. He was not so much a virtuoso as a good
craftsman, and as he said in another context *craft is al who so that
do it kan* (E 2016). But this only places him among the great
majority of English poets. The exceptions are few and such specialists as Tennyson and Swinburne and Robert Bridges are
usually regarded with suspicion, as though a high degree of
technical excellence or a marked devotion to it argues a deficiency
of inspiration or a thinness of matter. It is often objected even
of Milton that the constant richness of his rhythms can be a dis-
traction and sometimes out of harmony with what is being said.
A steady level of competence is preferred by readers of narrative
verse to displays of virtuosity: and this is what Chaucer gives.

None the less there are times when Chaucer dons the flowing
purple or spreads his wings just a little as though to demonstrate
what he can do when occasion arises. These displays of *maistrye,*
in which *art poetical* is plainly *shewed,* are easily recognized.
They are planned enhancements of the narrative in which they
occur or special exhibits, as in some of the shorter poems. They
are done with an air, and with manifest success. Some of the

3. "Chaucer's 'Good Ear,'" *R.E.S.* xxiii (1947), 20 ff., reprinted in
Essays on Middle English Literature, pp. 139-48.

prominent examples have been collected in the preceding chapter. There are others, less noticeable because shorter, which are seemingly spontaneous and appear as it were casually. Each of us has his favorites. There is

  The fresshe beautee sleeth me sodeynly,   A 1118

already mentioned; the simple dignity of

  Almighty and al merciable queene,   ABC 1

with it repetition of *al-*;

  Dusked his eyen two and failled breeth,   A 2806

where the important word has the metrically strongest position; the pathetic diminuendo of

  And hope is lasse and lasse alway, Pandare, *Tr.* IV 578

and the trochaic movement of

  Whoso me seeth, he seeth sorwe al at onys,
  Peyne, torment, pleynte, wo, distresse;   *Tr.* IV 841-42

the picturesque swiftness of

  Pekke hem vp right as they growe and ete hem in, B 4157

and the humorous echo in

  And sikerly she had a likerous eye,   A 3244

and the slightly frivolous *Lat take a cat* (H 175). And a hundred more, constant reminders of his Good Ear and confident skill.

 This then is the craftsman of verse—

  It nedeth me nat the longe[r] to forbise.

For him the craft was not so long to learn; he seems to have had it almost from the start, by a kind of instinct. ("When is a craft not a craft? When it's a gift.") He knew the whole diapason, all the stops from vox humana to full organ, to suit the needs of his subjects. He could be casual, even careless, he could be subtle and cunning—as the occasion required. There are times when he revealed the conscious artist (though not self-conscious) and times when he was willing to let things take their natural course. Felicities came easily, or, if not, he was content to press on with a second-best. In short, his versification has the same uneven qualities—from the highest on down—as his whole work.

This is most evident in the *Troilus*, where Chaucer employs all the stops. The handling of both line and stanza plainly reflects the liveliness of the first two Books, and is in contrast to that of Book v, which is more subdued in keeping with its different tone. Only in a few lyric or dramatic passages of Book v is there any conspicuous variation. For example, in the fifteen stanzas of the *Litera Troili* (v 1317 ff.) the meter is appropriately even and formal, the line unit almost always preserved, and 'irregular' lines infrequent. Criseyde's shorter reply (1590-1631), in which she seems genuinely sincere, although she has already *falsed Troilus* (1053) is similarly restrained, with only one little outbreak of impatience in the first stanza. But in her self-confessional lament (1054-85) she is more agitated and the lines show it; and Chaucer ends the speech with an echo rime which is like a poignant pun:

> *And gilteles, I woot wel, I yow leve;*
> *But al shal passe; and thus take I my leve.*   v 1084-85

And again, in Troilus' farewell to her, when he is reconciled to his loss, the meter is quiet and regular, with only six run-on lines in its seven stanzas. Its closing couplet also has a special rime:

> *But, trewely, Criseyde, swete may,*
> *Whom I have ay with al my myght yserved,*
> *That ye thus doon, I have it nat deserved.*   v 1720-22

The *ubi sunt* stanza (v 218-24) is lyrically embellished by the resemblance of the a-rimes *dere clere* (close *e*) and the b-rimes *where were teere* (open *e*). The apostrophes in 540 ff., *O paleys . . . O hous . . . O paleys . . . O thow lanterne . . . O paleys . . . O paleys . . . O ryng . . . O cause* include a twofold repetition of *whilom*, picked up two stanzas later. Similar are the *Whi . . . Whi nyl . . . Whi wol* of v 40 ff., answered by *But why* in the next stanza. Then there are the familiar anaphoras *Swych fin . . .* and *Lo here . . .* at the end. The interweaving of two formulas in v 1373-79 is reminiscent of BD 599 ff. and KtT 2924 ff. Here they are *Myn eyen . . . arn woxen—My song in—myn ese ek woxen—My joie in . . .*; then one waits until

> *I kan sey yow naught ellis*

to complete the *in* construction—

> *naught ellis*
> *But torned is, . . .*

Here the editors have been put to it for punctuation. Both Skeat and Root have wrongly a full stop after 1376, in the middle of the series, and thus interrupt its calculated flow. Chaucer's apology for Criseyde (v 1093-99) is notable for the tripartite division of the stanza, and has also a good nine-syllable line beginning with the special emphasis of *Forther*. In the summarizing analysis of Criseyde's character,

> *Charitable, estatlich, lusty, and fre,*   v 823

the first four feet are inverted (trochaic), the natural pause after *Charitable* makes for a trisyllabic (dactylic) foot, and the hiatus *lusty, and* affords a dramatic pause. A nine-syllable all-trochaic line follows:

> *Tendre herted, slydynge of corage.*   v 825

The early part of Book III is Chaucer's own, but at l. 239 he returns to Boccaccio as Pandarus *in a sobre wyse* makes his apology for acting as go-between—his own self-justification and the poet's to the reader—and lectures Troilus on the sin of boasting. Pandarus is as usual diffuse (and aware of it; cf. 295 f.) but firm and in only one stanza (316-22, not from Boccaccio) rhetorical. The versification is appropriately firm. But when Troilus replies (360-85), he is confused and almost incoherent and the stanzas run together, until at 386 ff. he recovers his poise and answers Pandarus point by point. One would like to think here that the verse betrays Troilus's excitement: one must at least say that the lines move smoothly through the complicated syntax. So later, through all the talk about Horaste and jealousy and Criseyde's reflections (from Boethius) on the unstableness of joy, the verse keeps its natural even pace, as Chaucer builds up sus-

pense and Criseyde seems reluctant—until Troilus swoons from
nervous excitement, and then the meter picks up. So again in
Book IV, when Criseyde swoons from grief and Troilus prepares to commit suicide, it is only in his farewell to Troy, to his
father and mother, and to her (1205-11) that the verse reflects
his emotion. And again, when, in bed, Criseyde argues for her
practical plan (1254 ff.) and Troilus though mistrustful replies
patiently, the verse keeps pace with the plain language—until she
answers him *with a sik* (1527) and with her great oath by all the
greater and lesser gods, and then the verse seems to rise above
plainness—

> *And thow, Symois, that as an arwe clere*
> *Thorugh Troie rennest ay downward to the se . . .*
> *That thow retourne bakward to thi welle.* IV 1548-53

At the end of Book III Chaucer takes leave of Venus and
Cupid: the lovers are *in lust and in quiete* and their story as a
love story is finished. At the same time, and significantly, he says
that the Nine Muses will no longer be his guide:

> *I kan no more, but syn that ye wol wende,*
> *Ye heried ben for ay withouten ende—* III 1812-13

a blessing and dismissal. Still the other half of Troilus' double
sorrow remains, so in the third stanza of Book IV he explains:

> *For how Criseyde Troilus forsook . . .*
> *Moot hennesforth ben matere of my book.* IV 15-17

He now invokes all three Furies—only one of them at the beginning of the poem—and Mars also, to help finish *This ilke
ferthe book*, which is to show forth

> *the losse of lyf and love yfeere*
> *Of Troilus.*

He requires however two Books and 3500 lines to make an end.
It will not be denied that these last two books drag, in spite
of some fine passages. Nor will it quite do to say that Chaucer
is concerned to ring every change on the pathos of the linger-
ing tale. And it will be recalled that more than 60 per cent of
Book IV and 70 per cent of Book V are straight out of Boccaccio.

Troilus and Criseyde in their several lamentations and letters show as great diffusion of speech as Pandarus himself and they both pick up his habit of using proverbs. There is little action and no suspense. Would it then be too rash to say that the poet's ease and accumulated facility in multiplying stanzas overran his first intention? While we admire this ease and facility we need not forget that they can be an artistic handicap, like the "equable iambics" of Morris' *Jason*. It was 'easier' to run on, with Boccaccio, than to condense, to describe Troilus' loss of love and life in the reasonable compass of *This ilke ferthe book*.

Miss Hammond sums up neatly: "We can find alliteration in Chaucer," she says, "but no such subtlety as Keats'

> *The dreary melody of bedded reeds*   [Endymion I 239]

... We can find skilful phrase-handling, but not such as Shelley's. Nor do we expect it. Chaucer is a master of the larger speech-unit which his narrative key requires, and no man working in his key has done better."[4] Chaucer had no need for the complex rhythms of Milton or the elaborate orchestration of line and stanza of Shelley and Swinburne, or of the artistic subtleties of Tennyson. Nor should we expect them. His business was to tell a story that would please a none too exigent audience, and for this he created a style and a method of versifying which were perfectly suited to his aim.

4. *English Verse between Chaucer and Surrey*, Durham, N. C., 1927, pp. 18-19.

APPENDIX 1. THE RHYTHMICAL OR FOUR-BEAT HERESY

THERE is a heresy—Professor Southworth[1] would call it a Myth—which holds that Chaucer's five-stress line was not five-stress at all and not iambic. Southworth's position is a natural development from his *PMLA* article cited above (p. 18 n.) and seems also to be related to Mr. C. S. Lewis' essay, "The Fifteenth-Century Heroic Line" in *Essays and Studies* XXIV, 1938, pp. 28-41. It is related somehow to the still vexed versification of Lydgate and the breakdown of English verse in the century following Chaucer. But its real origin lies in the common failure or unwillingness to recognize the difference between meter and rhythm, which appears now and then apropos of Milton's blank verse and has recently been brought forward by Professor Frye in his *Anatomy of Criticism*.[2]

This heresy actually dates back to the early nineteenth century, long before Child had explored the historical bearings of syllabic *e*. It seems to have appeared first in Dr. Nott's edition of Surrey and Wyatt.[3] Dr. Nott had his faults, pardonable at his date, but he grasped his nettle firmly. Chaucer's chief improvement, he says,

was that of dropping altogether the use of the Alexandrine line, and substituting the line of ten syllables in its stead. . . . But . . . he suffered it to retain in other respects the properties of the old Alexandrian verse. Like that it was divided by the old caesura into hemistichs; had the pause at the end, and was recited rhythmically. It was still what Lydgate called 'the verse of Cadence.' It is true that many of Chaucer's lines have the appearance of being pure Iambic Decasyllables. This

1. James G. Southworth, *Verses of Cadence*, Oxford, 1954.
2. Northrop Frye, *Anatomy of Criticism*, Princeton, 1957, pp. 251 ff. In a recent paper Mr. Lewis recognizes the distinction. See C. S. Lewis, "Metre," *Rev. of English Literature*, 1 (1960), 45-50.
3. Geo. Fred. Nott, *The Works of Henry Howard, Earl of Surrey and of Sir Thomas Wyatt the Elder*. London, 1815, 2 vols.; vol. 1, Dissertation, cxxxvii ff. Section IV, "Of Chaucer's versification—that his verses were Decasyllables, but rhythmical—of the use and importance of the caesura in rhythmical versification" (pp. clviii-clxiv).

however was the effect of accident. . . . It was the frequent occurrence
of these fortuitous Iambic lines that led Mr. Tyrwhitt, and before him
Mr. Urry, and the learned Mr. Morell, to believe that Chaucer's system of versification was altogether metrical. . . .

Should it be asked why so many Iambic lines are to be found in
Chaucer, the answer is obvious. Our language had become more compressed. Most of the words in common use had dropped their final
syllables, and monosyllables were multiplied.

In support of this opinion Dr. Nott compares Robert Man-
ning's continuation of Langtoft's *Chronicle* and instances a number of lines which look like Iambic Decasyllables but are not
intentionally such, and are "easily reducible to cadence or rhythm.
The case was otherwise with Chaucer. He used it uniformly, and
upon system. This admits of no doubt." The doctor now tran-
scribes the opening line of the General Prologue with his own
markings.

> *Whĕn thăt Aprìl* || *wĭth hĭs shōurĕs sòote* |
> *Thĕ drōught of Màrch* || *hăd pīerced tŏ thĕ ròote* |
> *And bāthĕd ĕvĕry vèin* || *ĭn sūch liqùour* |
> *Ŏf whĭch vīrtùe* || *ĕngēndĕrĕd ĭs thĕ flòur* |
> *Whĕn Zĕphĭrŭs èke* || *wĭth hĭs sōote brèath* |

and so on. One may note some inconsistencies here, but one gets
the general notion of how Dr. Nott thought the lines should
sound. He then goes on to offer his reasons. First, a large proportion of Chaucer's lines cannot be read as Iambic Decasyllables
"without doing the utmost violence to our language," but if read
properly they "are harmonious verses of cadence." And further,
if Chaucer had meant them as iambic "a slight transposition"
would have easily set them right. E. g.

In hèr ĭs hìgh bĕautè || *wĭthòutĕn prìde* Cant. Tales. 4522 [B 162]

has if so read "all the harmony that sort of versification aspires
to"; whereas if Chaucer had wanted a true iambic decasyllable he
would have written

> *In her high beauty is, withouten pride.*

(Manly, Robinson read *In hire is heigh beautee.*) Secondly, there
are many defective verses, inconsistent with metrical but not with

rhythmical versification. Thirdly, "a conclusive reason," the best manuscripts mark by point or by virgule how the minstrels should read Chaucer to their "mixed unlettered multitude, greedily drinking in the varied strains with wondering ears . . ." Extracts from sundry manuscripts now illustrate all this.

It would be as easy as it would be pointless to talk back to Dr. Nott. But he is worth quoting at some length because he antici- pated nearly all that the heretics have later maintained. Their variations of the theme must however be glanced at.

First, there is Legouis's doctoral dissertation.[4] Many lines can- not be scanned as iambic and are not divisible into five parts. The following lines should be read:

> *Without / en hyre / if it lay / in his might*   [A 538
> *And wel / I woot / as ye goon / by the weye*   [A 771
> *As great / as it were / for an al / e-stake*   [A 667
> *The reule / of Seint Maure / or of Seint / Beneit*   [A 173

They show a tendency (at least) towards the loose four-stress line which is called tumbling verse and which Spenser employed, for rustic effect, in the February and May Eclogues. Thus

> *Ah for pittie! wil ranke Winters rage*
> *These bitter blasts never ginne tasswage?*
> *The kene cold blowes through my beaten hyde,*
> *All as I were through the body gryde:*
> *My ragged rontes all shiver and shake,*
> *As doon high Towers in an earthquake.*   February
>
> *Is not thilke the mery moneth of May,*
> *When love-lads masken in fresh aray? . . .*
> *Tho gan shepheards swaines to looke aloft*
> *And leave to live hard, and learn to ligge soft. . . .*   May

Thus Legouis in 1896; but surely one would not now read Chaucer to this tune. The principle of this meter is four stresses with an irregular number of unstressed syllables. It goes back to

4. Emile Legouis, *Quomodo Edmundus Spenserus ad Chaucerem se fingens in Eclogis the Shepheardes calendar versum heroicum renovarit ac refecerit.* Paris, 1896. N.V.; not in L.C.; quoted by Albert H. Licklider, *Chapters on the Metric of the Chaucer Tradition,* Baltimore, 1910, pp. 19-20.

the alliterative Anglo-Saxon line; it appears in *Gammer Gurton's Needle*—

> *As Gammer Gurton, with many a wyde styche,*
> *Sat pesynge and patching of Hodg her mans briche,*

and it survives still for light verse, as in Thackeray's

> *This Mary was pore and in misery once,*
> *And she came to Mrs. Roney it's more than twelve monce.*

King James, in his *Reulis and Cautelis*, 1585, gave it its name of "Rouncefallis, or Tumbling verse" and recommended it for "flyting, or Invectives." It is what Dr. Nott calls rhythmical as opposed to metrical and what would be now called purely accentual meter. Spenser smoothed it—as he would—by reducing the number of unstressed syllables and thereby altered the tune. If in his archaizing he meant to suggest Chaucer it does not follow that he read all of Chaucer in this way.[5]

Mr. C. S. Lewis comes at the Chaucer problem historically. He observes that "nothing in their poetical experience had prepared the Englishmen of Chaucer's time" for our modern iambic decasyllable, and he asks two very interesting questions. "(1) Is it probable that Chaucer himself had caught the music of the modern decasyllabic and intended his countrymen to hear this music in his own verse? (2) Even if Chaucer did so intend, is it at all probable that they would have understood him? The first question I leave for the present unanswered." To the second he answers No.

If Chaucer meant his lines to be read as the modern scholar reads them, it is extremely likely that he was disappointed. Indeed, having begun his great poem with

> *Whán that Ápril with his shóures sóote,*

he was asking a good deal if he expected readers bred on the alliterative line, the octosyllabic, the *Horn* metre, and the metre of *Gamelyn*, to see at once that the poem was to go to the pattern if [i.e., of] 'And singing masons building roofs of gold.'[6]

5. Cf. R. M. Alden, *English Verse*, New York [1903], pp. 156-59. Later, p. 180, Alden notes the "close approach" of Spenser's use of it to the regular five-stress line.
6. *Essays and Studies*, pp. 31-32.

After submitting two more examples—

> *Whan Zéphirus éek · with his swéte bréeth*   [A 5
> *Bút a góvernòur · wýly and wíse—*   [B 3130

and conceding that "there are hundreds of lines in Chaucer that demand pure decasyllabic reading," he concludes: "I suspect that his verse was a precarious balance of different metrical forces. He himself knew how to read it aloud; but perhaps, even from the first, few others could read it exactly as he wished" (p. 39). To which it is perhaps enough to add that they could have learned from listening to him.

Professor Southworth echoes this. "Of one thing we can be certain. If Chaucer's prosody had differed as markedly from the English tradition as later nineteenth-century scholars seemed to think, he would not have been immediately popular. . . . If Chaucer were introducing the iambic decasyllable we should expect to find considerable resistance to his innovation and a delayed popularity; but we find none" (pp. 49, 50).

To supplement Mr. Lewis' few examples and for comparison with Dr. Nott's, here is Professor Southworth's reading of A 1-18 (pp. 66-67), omitting his musical notation.

> *Whán thăt Ápríl wĭth hĭs shóures sóote*
> *Thĕ dróghte ŏf Márch / hăth pércĕd tŏ thĕ róote*
> *Ănd báthĕd everў véyne / ĭn swĭch lĭcóur*
> *Óf whĭch vértŭ ĕngéndrĕd ĭs thĕ flóur*
> *Whán zéphĭrŭs éek wĭth hĭs swétee [sic] bréeth*
> *Ĭnspírĕd háth / ĭn everў hólt ănd héeth*
> *Thĕ téndrĕ cróppes / ănd thĕ yónge sónne*
> *Háth ĭn thĕ rám / hĭs hálf cóurs ўrónne*
> *Ănd smále fówelĕs / mákĕn mélŏdýe*
> *Thăt slépĕn ál thĕ nýght / wĭth ópĕn éye*
> *Sŏ príkĕth hém nătúre ĭn hĭr cŏrágĕs*
> *Thánne lóngĕn fólk / tŏ góon ŏn pílgrĭmágĕs*
> *Ănd pálmĕrĕs / fór tŏ sékĕn stráunge stróndĕs*
> *Tŏ férne hálwĕs / kŏwthe ĭn sóndrў lóndĕs*
> *Ănd spécĭallў frăm everў shírĕs énde*

Ŏf Éngelŏnd / tŏ Cáuntĕrbúrў thĕy wénde
Thĕ hólў blísfŭl mártŭr fór tŏ séke
Thăt hém hăth hólpĕn whán thăt théy wĕre séeke.

On this Southworth comments that the passage could be read
more subtly than he has indicated, "often with four or six stresses
rather than five"; that it has more iambs than the description
of the Prioress; that the skeptical may question his taking
straunge and *ferne* as monosyllables, and also *half*. In fact, five
of the eighteen lines do have as marked four stresses (1, 2, 7, 15,
16) and may be taken as rhythmical rather than metrical; and
two of the eighteen (5, 12) have six stresses by virtue of the accent
on their first words *Whan, Thanne*. The remaining eleven of the
eighteen (a high proportion) are taken as five-stress and four of
these (3, 10, 11, 18) are quite regular metrically; two others (6,
17) Southworth makes regular by means of an unexpected stress
on *hath* and *for* (thus betraying the traditional, i.e., metrical
habit); and likewise he makes line 4 regular, with trochaic substitution in the first two feet and with very surprising stresses
on *Of* and *is*. In short, Professor Southworth's marking reveals
an unacknowledged confusion between meter and rhythm; and
this confusion in the marking of A 1-18 is in striking contrast to
the dozen or so examples on his preceding pages (58-65) where
he is concerned to exhibit the difference between the metrical
iambic base and the rhythmical sound of the lines. It invalidates
the whole of his position and amounts to arguing in a circle,
counterclockwise. For the first question should be: What was
Chaucer's metrical base? Was it five iambs or was it four stresses
with an unprescribed number of unstressed syllables? Not till
this question is answered can the rhythm of the lines be recognized—the rhythm being, as always, the resolution of conflict
between scansion and the natural prose enunciation. Professor
Southworth's feeling for the sound of Chaucer's verse, is, so far
as I can infer it, not very different from yours and mine. We may
part company over any number of details, but a sort of general
agreement is all that can be expected for reading both mediæval
and modern and even contemporary verse. None of us is entirely

consistent; the poet himself may not represent perfectly the rhythm he heard and hoped the reader would hear. But the issue now is not the rhythm of Chaucer's lines; it is his metrical system, the pattern in his mind and his appropriate variations of it.

Historically considered one might assume that the common native four-beat pattern would be Chaucer's starting point and that he modified this in the direction of a five-beat iambic movement, and such seems to be Mr. Lewis' view and probably Professor Southworth's: a hesitant compromise. But it would be a considerable derogation of Chaucer's intelligence that he had no clear notions of meter, no system. That he had a standard is plain from his prayer at the end of the *Troilus*—

> *So prey I God that non myswrite the,*
> *Ne the mysmetre for defaute of tonge.*

Here *tonge* is an echo rime to *oure tonge* two lines above: the latter is 'our language,' the former 'our way of speaking it.' English may be miswritten because of dialectal differences and because of uncertainties of spelling. His poem might be mismetered by faulty spelling or careless copying which would misrepresent the meter. Chaucer makes the same point in his words to Adam Scrivener.

The question is put in another form by Professor Frye, with full though not quite explicit awareness of our problem.

A four-stress line seems to be inherent in the structure of the English language. It is the prevailing rhythm of the earlier poetry . . . ; it is the common rhythm of popular poetry in all periods, of ballads and of most nursery rhymes. . . . The iambic pentameter provides a field of syncopation in which stress and metre can to some extent neutralize one another. If we read any iambic pentameters 'naturally,' giving the important words the heavy accent that they do have in spoken English, the old four-stress line stands out in clear relief against its metrical background. Thus: . . .

The passages submitted are well chosen, the first four lines of Hamlet's "To be, or not to be" speech and the first five lines of *Paradise Lost*. But there are other passages which would not serve so well. Try, for example a few lines later in Hamlet's speech (III. 1, 70-83) :

> *For* who *would* bear *the* whips *and* scorns *of* time,
> *The* op*pressor's* wrong, *the* proud *man's* con*tumely,*
> *The* pangs *of* dis*priz'd* love, *the* law's *de*lay,
> *The* in*solence of* off*ice, and the* spurns
> *That* pat*ient* mer*it of the* un*worthy* takes,
> *When* he *him*self might *his qui*e*tus* make
> *With a* bare bod*kin?* Who *would* far*dels* bear,
> *To* grunt *and* sweat *under a* weary life,
> *But that the* dread *of* some*thing after* death,
> *The* un*discovered* coun*try from whose* bourn
> No tra*veller re*turns, puz*zles the* will
> *And* makes *us* rath*er* bear *the* ills *we* have
> *Than* fly *to* oth*ers that we* know *not* of ?
> *Thus* con*science does make* cowa*rds of us* all; . . .

Of these fourteen lines five have five rhetorical emphases, four have four, and four have three. The sixth line would have either five or four depending on whether one emphasized "might." So in *Paradise Lost* I, 6-16:

> Sing, Hea*venly* Muse, *that, on the* se*cret top*
> *Of* Or*eb, or of* Sin*ai, didst in*spire
> *That* shep*herd who* first taught *the* cho*sen* seed
> *In the* be*ginning how the* heav*ens and* earth
> Rose *out of* Chaos: or, *if* Si*on* hill
> *De*light *thee* more, *and* Si*loa's* brook *that* flowed
> Fast *by the* or*acle of* God, *I* thence
> *In*voke *thy* aid *to my* ad*ven*t*urous* song,
> *That with* no mid*dle* flight *in*tends *to* soar
> *A*bove *the* A*onian* mount, *while it pur*sues
> Things *unat*temp*ted* yet *in* prose *or* rhyme.

Of these eleven lines five have five rhetorical emphases, three have four, and two have three. The seventh line would have either four or five according as one emphasized "I" or not. There is little profit however in this sort of competition, unless to warn against facile generalization.

The really challengeable statement is that "A four-stress line seems to be inherent in the structure of the English language." One should rather say, not so much in the structure of English as in the ear of Western man. For the four-beat unit occurs not only in popular English verse, but in popular Latin (*Ecce Caesar nunc triumphans* . . .), in the Romance octosyllabics and, in its way, in the French Alexandrine, as well as in nearly all popular music (marches and dance music, including the waltz). But the decasyllable is not a popular but a sophisticated, a literary form; and obviously ten is not readily divisible into four. That the decasyllable may *appear* to have sometimes a four-beat movement there are two good and sufficient reasons: (1) the need for relief from the monotony of consistently repeated iambs, and (2) the number of unemphatic monosyllables and of polysyllables with secondary accent. These two work together to afford variations which are both natural and inevitable. Together they support rather than contradict the five-stress iambic pattern. To argue otherwise is to reverse logic. No one has ever reckoned the proportion of purely iambic lines in English verse to those with normal variations: the figures would prove little beyond the fact that (as every one has said) the line of five iambs recurs often enough to preserve the basic pattern and to render the variations agreeable and acceptable. Even the heretics grant that in Chaucer they occur by "hundreds." The apparent four-beat lines do not testify to anything inherent in our language, they merely show how many lines tend, by virtue of the principle of variation, to have only four rhythmic emphases—rhythmic when read as prose. It is therefore confusing to be told that these lines, "standing out in clear relief against the metrical background," are due to something inherent in the structure of English, or even to something (as Professor Frye implies but does not say) in our general inherent feeling for rhythm; and it is misleading because it suggests that a four-beat rhythm is something which imposes itself on the metrical background and is therefore an element in the rhythmic principle of the 'pentameter.'

To come back now to the beginning, the distinction between meter and rhythm. The meter, being abstract, does not determine the rhythm, nor the rhythm the meter. They interweave, with mutual influence. One encroaches on the other to their mutual advantage: and this Professor Frye recognizes, when he writes, on a later page (271) that in

Ay, but to die, and go we know not where,   Meas f Meas

"We can hear of course the metrical rhythm [pattern], an iambic pentameter spoken as a four-stress line."

The weakness of Professor Southworth's position is due in part to his dual use of the word *rhythmical*—now in the sense of prose rhythm, the sound of verse as determined by its natural or rhetorical delivery, and now (after Dr. Nott) as a term for the four-beat native meter.[7] This confusion, along with his thesis that -*e* was silent in Chaucer's verse, precludes his recognizing the theoretical iambs of the meter and makes his scansions yield only a series of "spondees, pyrrhics, amphibrachs, and dactyls in various combinations, and too frequently to permit our calling the verse iambic pentameter" (p. 65), and forces him to posit a 'rhythmical' base which came from the older four-stress meter and is at the same time 'rhythmical' because it conforms to the natural or rhetorical rhythm of prose. What is more, he cannot be consistent, for he places an accent over *in* (*Entuned in hir nose,* A 123) and over *was* (*frenssh of Paris was to hire unknowe,* A 126) and over *up* and *hir* (*fille up on hir brest,* A 131), and over *In* (*In curtesye,* A 132), and over *is* (*engendered is the flour,* A 4), and over *hir*

7. Professor Southworth is not entirely clear on this point. He speaks (p. 49; cf. also p. 57) of "the basic similarity in the rhythms of Chaucer and *Piers Plowman*," and he says (p. 52) that Gascoigne "probably erred in thinking of Chaucer's verse as four-stressed." He grants that "Chaucer's problem, therefore, was to preserve the basic English rhythm, increase the vocabulary, regularize the line, and yet give it the fluidity possessed by French and Italian" (p. 51). His confusion is plain also in his approval of Professor Van Doren: that "the only real stresses in a line are the rhetorical stresses. It is easily possible to manipulate the reading of Chaucer's verses so that there are five rhetorical stresses in the line" (p. 54). This I would vigorously deny. Some lines of Chaucer do have five rhetorical stresses; many of them do not, and no amount of manipulation can put them there. What one maintains is that the metrical pattern has place for five stresses. The beauty of a line is its modulation away from the fixity of meter.

(*in hir corages,* A 11), and over *for* (*palmeres for to seken,* A 13, and *for to seke,* A 17). These details are from pp. 64-67; they look very much like willing concessions to the repudiated iamb.[8]

8. Here and there Southworth notices the use of the virgule and superior point in certain Chaucer manuscripts, as in those of Hoccleve and Lydgate. "It can occur anywhere" (p. 46); "It is, therefore, a rhetorical and not a metrical mark" (p. 62).—It is possible that some day some one will discover the significance of these scribal marks, but until then one can only say that they follow no readily discernible consistent principle.

THE CY Prologue and Tale raise several questions which a close look at the scansion may help to answer.

The poem comes late in the series of Tales. The appearance of two new figures when the Pilgrims are so near Canterbury has suggested that the whole incident was an afterthought and therefore Chaucer had a special reason for its inclusion in the Tales. The structure of the poem is peculiar in that the Prologue is partly of the nature of a link and partly of a Prologue in the usual sense. When the Yeoman begins his tale, according to the rubric, he seems to be talking about the Canon who rode with him, but in Pars Secunda the tale is about another canon who the Yeoman insists is different but whom he seems to confuse with the first. And the conclusion—*Considereth sires* (1388-1481)—is a general attack on alchemy rather above the pitch of our Yeoman. Then there is the direct address to the *chanons religious* (992) whom the speaker warns against harboring a Judas in their convent. The Yeoman with his rattling volubility in the Prologue and Pars Prima seems to have a character of his own, but when he settles into his tale about the other canon his tone and style are somewhat different—as they should be, as they are for example in the Prologue and Tale of the Pardoner. The versification of the whole poem, however, is uniform in its alternation or interchange of easy smoothness and apparent carelessness.

The familiar variations of Chaucer's heroic line may be passed over without comment—unless they begin to look like license. This becomes of course a matter of proportion. Consider the number of lines which begin with a weak stress: *He was* 565, *And in* 569, *For he* 575, *But it* 579, *Out of* 589, *Which that* 591, *He is* 596, *He hath* 605, *He is* 613, *Vn to* 628, *That of* 632, *As in* 634, *It is* 635, and so on and on. Several of these have a weak stress elsewhere within the line. Along with this goes the metrical padding with little words: *for to be* 573, *for to kepe* 578, *for to seen* 579, *It for to doon* 679, and so on, as well as the convenient use of *vn to* where *to* would suffice; *til that* 570, *whan that* 582, *Which that* 591, *Til that* 624, *If that* 638, *whiche that* 755, and so on. It is the too ready and frequent reliance on these handy helps which requires notice. In themselves they are conventional and innocent, if they are not overworked. They end in producing a large number of lines with only three or two or even one rhetorical stress, where the sense does not call for such emphasis. Effective are

He was of foom al flekked as a pye	565
I demed hym som chanoun for to be	573
But it was ioye for to seen hym swete	579
Syn that thy lord is of so heigh prudence	630
By cause that I am a lewed man.	787

But compare on the other side:

By cause that I wolde yow atake	585
Which that to riden with yow is ful fayn	591
Which were ful hard for any that is heere	606
Al that I haue in my possessioun	612
By cause of which men sholde him reuerence	631
As in effect to hym so moot I go	634
When we been ther as we shul exercise	750
Of thynges whiche that we werche vp on,	755

and so on till

Vn to that day in which that I shal crepe	1045
With his brother and that is for to sayn,	1437

and for sharp contrast

Goth walketh forth and bryngeth a chalk stoon	
For I wol make it of the same shap.	1207-8

Inversion is frequently an asset, as in

His hat heng at his bak doun by a laas	574
A quod the yeman heere shal arise game	703
That feele I wel what so any man seith,	711

and later on

Thogh poure I be crafty thow shalt me fynde	1290
He semed freendly to hem that knewe hym noght	1302

(that is, if one takes *semed* as monosyllabic; else an anapest).
But as often as not the inversion comes as a surprise or the stress
is forced onto a weak syllable:

God it amende I kan seye yow namore	651
Which this yeman spak for suspecioun	686
He shal no good han that hym may suffise	831
In my visage for fumes dyuerse	1098
Of this teyne with outen any drede	1229
A mannes myrthe it wol turne in to grame.	1403

When two consecutive feet are trochaic the reader's ear is a little
disconcerted——

Yet forgat I to maken rehersaille	852
Goddes blessyng and his modres also	1243
For to come to theffect of his desir	1261
Al his werkyng nas but fraude and deceit.	1367

But finally, as if to make amends for all, Chaucer finished the
Tale with a flourish of two dactyls, two spondees, and a trochee:

God sende euery trewe man boote of his bale.	1481

These examples are illustrative, not exhaustive. They are set
down not as flaws, but to show that their frequency is part of the
whole picture. On the other hand, there are many sequences of
smooth and regular lines which display Chaucer at his best—
for instance the opening passage, 657 ff., the beginning of Pars
Secunda (972 ff.), and others with only slight interruptions.

When the Yeoman spills out his list of technical terms *vn to
oure craft apertenyng* (785) there are a good many lines which
are hardly expected to scan, yet Chaucer contrives with remarkable skill to make them sound metrical and intermingles them
with fairly regular lines to fortify the pattern. Scattered throughout, however, and especially towards the end are lines which out
of context read like prose and in context seriously blur the pattern.
Of these a fairly full (though not complete) list is necessary.
Some are rougher than others, and of course individual readers
will differ, but the mass is noteworthy and cannot be paralled
elsewhere in Chaucer.

In the suburbes of town quod he	657
Whil this yeman was thus in his talkyng	684
Which this yeman spak for suspecioun	686
Of mennes speche euere hadde this chanon	687
To his yeman to herknen al his sawe	691
I koude neuere leue it in no wise	714
That I haue no good wher that euere I fare	733
To haue hir felawes in peyne and disese	747
Of thynges whiche that we werche vp on	755
As on fyue or sixe ounces may wel be	756
And in an erthen pot how put is al	761
And salt yput in and also papeer	762
That of the eyr myghte passe out no thyng	767
Is lost also which we vp on it leye	783
He shal no good han that hym may suffise	831
And euery man that hath oght in his cofre	836
Ascaunce that craft is so light to lere	838
As in effect he shall fynde it al oon	847
Somme seyde it was long on the fir makyng	922
Somme seyde nay it was on the blowyng	923
Straw quod the thridde ye been lewed and nyce	925
Of thise perils I wol be war eft soone	933
Plukke vp youre hertes and beeth glad and blithe	937
And telle forth my tale of the chanon	1020
That broghte this preest to confusioun	1021
And kithed to me so greet gentillesse	1054
Noght wiste this preest with whom that he delte	1074
Wher fore to go to the conclusioun	1082
In my visage for fumes dyuerse	1098
Of metals which ye han herd me reherce	1099
Consumed and wasted han my reednesse	1100
Now tak heed of this chanons cursednesse	1101
Of his bosom and shewed it the preest	1118
And make it as good siluer and as fyn	1128
This preest at this cursed chanons biddyng	1144
Shul werche al thyng which that shal here be do	1155
And ther inne put was of siluer lymaille	1162

And leyde it aboue vp on the myddeward	1190
Of the crosselet and blew wel afterward	1191
I ne wol nat been out of youre presence	1215
Of an ingot as I shal yow deuyse	1223
He shoop his ingot in lengthe and in brede	1228
He putte his hand in and took vp a teyne	1240
With that oother which that now siluer is	1257
This preest hym bisieth in al that he kan	1258
For to come to theffect of his desir	1261
And for a countenance in his hande he bar	1264
To hym anon and his poudre caste in	1272
Is ther any coper her inne seyde he	1292
To thentente that men may be war ther by	1306
He putte this ounce of coper in the crosselet	1308
Vnwityng this preest of his false craft	1320
To this chanoun for this ilke receit	1366
Of my craft for I wolde it kept were cloos	1369
By the dragon Mercurie and noon oother	1438
Lat no man bisy hym this art for to seche	1442
Thanne conclude I thus sith that god of heuene	1472
As for to werken any thyng in contrarie.	1477

I repeat, it is not that all these lines are bad or that they resist scansion—some of them are very good when read for their rhetorical effect, regardless of meter—it is that their continual recurrence disturbs the ear conditioned to metrical regularity and the intelligence because the prose rhythm is inadequately subdued to the prepared pattern. Strict conformity is never desirable but closer agreement between meter and rhythm is ordinarily expected.

A few examples on the other side will even the balance and point up the contrast. The Narrator says in the Prologue with his characteristic modesty that he first studied the Canon's dress and

> *whan I longe hadde auysed me*
> *I demed hym som chanoun for to be*
> *His hat heeng at his bak doun by a laas*   572-74

The editors, following the El scribe and some others, read *hadde long*. This is certainly smoother but it is not better because it reduces the emphasis on *longe*, gained by the inversion. The false stress on *for* in the next line is atoned for by the inversions of *heeng at* and *down by*. Again, the false emphasis is corrected by the spondaic foot:

> *Yet is it fals and ay we han good hope*   678

only to be followed by a slip backward in the next line: *It for to doon.*

Again:

> *Whil this yeman was thus in his talkyng*
> *This chanoun drough hym neer and herd al thing*
> *Which this yeman spak for suspecioun*
> *Of mennes speche eure hadde this chanoun.*   684-87

The repetition of *this* belongs to the style of over-simple narration. It is not infrequent elsewhere in the poem; cf. 1144-47. It is particularly feeble in 687, where *he* would have been enough, but probably the necessity of riming is to be blamed. In 686 one hesitates momentarily, inasmuch as *yeman* may be accented on either syllable, between *Which thís* and *Which this*, and the latter brings three emphatic monosyllables together: *al thing Which*. And *Which* is right, as is proved by the pause after *spak*. One is then left with *for suspecioun*—and an anapest. The alternative

> *Which thís yemán spak fór suspecioùn*

is so much inferior that there can be no question. (Yet Robinson reads *Which that*.) Thus Chaucer delights us with his cunning, only to trip us in the next line: *mennes or mennés*?

Anapests or near-anapests are a little more frequent in CYT than elsewhere: e.g., *lewed and nyce* 647, *felawes in peyne* 747, *a bolle or a panne* 1210, *For the loue of God* (edd. and some MSS omit *the*) 1351, *Which is that* 1455, and

> *Consumed and wasted han my reednesse*
> *Now tak heed of this chanons cursednesse*   1100-01

(where one says *Consuméd* for the sake of the parallel *wasted*;

and the anapest can be avoided only by forcing a stress on *of*), and

> *And leyde it aboue vp on the myddeward*   1190
> *And for a countenance in his hand he bar.*   1264

The same mingling of good and less good as in 684-87 (above) appears in

> *Sitte we doun and lat vs myrie make*
> *And whan that this chanons bechen cole*
> *Was brent al the lemaille out of the hole*
> *In to the crosselet fil anon adoun.*   1195-98

The first is a good nine-syllable line (or possibly *Sittẻ* is better?) and the second is not, if one says *Ánd whan thát this*. But the natural way is *And whán that thís*, leaving a Lydgate line. But the beauty of the passage begins with the pause after *brent*; then two choriambs (so to say) *all the lemaille* and *out of the hole* and another *In to the crosse*——and then the plunge: *fil anon adoun.*

Other Lydgate lines are

> *And whils that the preest couched bisily*   1179

(Robinson without MS authority reads *whiles*; Globe *whylẹs* as monosyllable and *couchede*),

> *And whils that the preest wiped his face*   1188

(Robinson *whiles*; Globe *whylẹs*),

> *This noble craft and this subtiltee.*   1247

This last word occurs four times in the poem: 844 and 1371, where it is trisyllabic, and 620 and here, where, as elsewhere in Chaucer, it seems to count as four syllables.

Some of the metrical license has an equivalent in the style. Note the grammatical inversion of *come vs to* 867 and *seyde his maister to* 1449, both for the rime's sake, and *it in hise handes nam* 1297. For a fair sample of the almost too easy style, to put alongside the passages already cited, take

> *Sire quod the preest it shal be doon ywis*
> *He bad his seruant fecchen hym this thyng*
> *And he al redy was at his biddyng*

> *And wente hym forth and cam anon agayn*
> *With this quyk siluer shortly for to sayn*
> *And took thise ounces thre to the chanoun*
> *And he hem leyde faire and wel adoun*
> *And bad the seruant coles for to brynge*
> *That he anon myghte go to his werkynge.*   1107-15

And for a sample of complex but clumsy syntax take

> *And this chanoun right in the mene while*
> *Al redy was this preest eft to bigile*
> *And for a countenance in his hande he bar*
> *An holwe stikke taak keep and be war*
> *In the ende of which an ounce and namoore*
> *Of siluer lymaille put was as bifore*
> *Was in his cole and stopped with wex weel*
> *For to kepe in his lymaille euery deel.*   1262-69

There are two canons in the poem and they work by different methods: the Yeoman's Canon who tried worthless formulas and the other, a hundredfold more subtle (1091), who used sleight of hand. The Yeoman insists that they are different (1088 ff.) but he blends the two when he says (as though he were the poet) that it bores him *to ryme* of the latter and at the same time blames the latter for the ruin of his complexion as he had blamed the former back in 665 ff. Then the Yeoman confounds them when he says (1173 ff.) that he wishes to get back at the second canon —who is only a figure in the story of Pars Secunda—and is introduced as such (1012 ff.)—with whom he has apparently had no personal contact. Finally, there is a real difference in tone between the Yeoman's condemnation of alchemists, which is grounded on his own experience (720-47 and *passim*) and on which he is unwilling to be quoted (642-43), and the more elaborate repudiation at the end (1388-1482). Being himself uneducated the Yeoman vouches for his

> *That that is ouerdoon it wol nat preue*   645

by citing *clerkes*, whereas at the end he remembers *Bayard the blynde* and quotes Arnoldus de Villa Nova and the little anecdote

of Plato's disciple, and is credited (wrongly) with knowledge of
the Pseudo-Aristotelian *Secreta Secretorum*.

All these diverse elements, the uneven styles and irregular
versification, and certain inconsistencies including the direct address to *worshipful chanons religious* (992) and *sires* (1388),
might be accounted by assuming that the nucleus, Pars Secunda,
with the concluding denunciation of alchemists and all their ways,
was composed rapidly, even hurriedly, for a special occasion (as
was partly suggested by Manly) and to give expression to some
strong personal feeling. Chaucer's knowledge of the subject—at
least of its technical jargon—can be explained in various ways
without supposing that he had himself been tricked by some false
canon. Yet there is a force and energy in the closing comminatory
lines which makes them more convincing and more serious than
in Chaucer's usual reproofs of contemporary evils. After which
he smiles at himself with the double image, *a poynt*, of the speaking Yeoman and the poet, pen in hand, as the Pilgrim reporter.
The prayer in the last line is conventional, but it has a further
point: *boote of his bale*—IF he be *a trewe man*. The subsequent
invention of the incident at Boughton-under-Blee would give *my
tale* a place in the Canterbury pilgrimage; but the confusion of
the two canons stands as witness of imperfect adaptation and as
evidence of haste.

This may be a desperate hypothesis. It is supported by another
consideration. Scholars are agreed that the whole poem is 'late.'
Some of it is in Chaucer's best and most mature manner. The
irregularities of versification in some places, beside manifest skill
in others, may be explained as a conscious freeing and loosening
of metrical standards comparable to what one finds in the blank
verse of Shakespeare's later plays or, on a different level, to the
differences between the versification of *Paradise Lost* and that of
Paradise Regained. What sounds and looks like careless and hasty
writing, the iambic pattern giving way to the freedom of prose,
may thus be deliberate, or at the least an experiment. Or, on the
other hand, if the poem was written for the *Canterbury Tales* and
is, as it seems to be, all of a piece from l. 554 to l. 1481, it might
be thought—perhaps an even more desperate hypothesis—that

what look like faults in style and versification are really a kind of characterization of the Yeoman: he would talk like that. And so he did part of the time, though at other times Chaucer's habitual skill intruded. The frequent superimposition of prose rhythm over meter would thus be a display of *art poetical*.

After all, the CY Prologue and Tale *is* different. Its best qualities are mixed with other qualities not found elsewhere in a way that raises unusual questions and calls for unusual answers. The peculiarities of versification are but one aspect—here the 'inciting moment' provoking corroborative speculation.

APPENDIX 3· METRICAL REVISION IN THE *TROILUS*?

THE relationships of the *Troilus* MSS are very complex, but it is agreed that they fall into three main groups, α, β, γ, of which α represents the earliest version. Unfortunately only one MS, Ph, is consistently α. No one MS is consistently β throughout, though J is β up to the last two thousand odd lines. On the other hand three of the 'best' MSS are consistently γ, Cl, Cp, Hı. All the rest are 'mixed' or 'corrupt' or both, in varying proportions. It is agreed also that βγ represent some revision by Chaucer; but whether they represent two revisions (and if so which is the later) or only one, is a matter of dispute: McCormick and Root regard β, Skeat and Robinson γ, as containing Chaucer's final text. One kind of revision is obvious: the α MS Ph has the hymn to Love at the end of Book III (1744-71), the soliloquy on free will in Book IV (953-1085), and the *Teseida* stanzas towards the end of Book V (1807-27) on inset leaves. These three passages were presumably added by Chaucer to his first version and are so recognized by everyone. The other 'revisions' consist of variants within a line and occasionally of several lines together, which are valuable for the classification of the MSS; yet this is true mainly, though not exclusively, as distinguishing α from βγ. Otherwise it is never easy to tell authorial revision from scribal variants.

One would very much like to know, for the present study, if the variants reveal any changes made by Chaucer for metrical reasons. The answer is not simple. For example, for

> *That the Grekes as the deth him dredde*   I 483

(so Root and Robinson), α (followed by Skeat and Globe) reads *That al(le) the Grekes*. Did Chaucer deliberately alter his first version to make a nine-syllable line? In I 492 Root and Globe read *I kan;* but the γ MSS Cp, Cl, Hı, followed by Skeat and Robinson, read *can I*. Which is the 'better' metrically? Which is Chaucer's? Similarly, in I 495 γ has *rede I* (so Globe and Root) but

Skeat and Robinson *I rede*. Examples of this kind are legion. A more interesting case is

"*Thow seist wel," quod Pandarus, "and now I hope.* 1939

This is Root's text, following Cp, Cl, H₁ (the best of γ) and J (β); but the other MSS have *Pandar(e)*, followed by Skeat, Globe, and Robinson. If these γ mss and the β J represent authorial revision, then Chaucer wrote a hypermetrical line deliberately. But the editors, except Root, have thought otherwise; they have corrected Chaucer's revision—or, as they would probably say, the scribes' error. Just before this, 1938 has *nevere more whil I live* (so edd.), but α has *whil þat*. Did Chaucer first write *whil that* and later strike out *that* to make *more* disyllabic and so more emphatic?—But certainly it is unprofitable to pursue such questions.

On the other hand, in the Bidding Prayer in the Proem to Book i, a passage to which Chaucer must have devoted particular care, α reads (24-28 with minor var.):

> *Remembre you of olde passid hevynesse*
> *For goddis love, and on adversitee*
> *That other suffren, thynke how somtyme þat ye*
> *Fownde how love durst you displese,*
> *Or ellis ye wonne hym with to grete ease*

This looks like rough work, a first draft. Although the metrical irregularities could easily have been tidied up, Chaucer rewrote the lines:

> *Remembreth yow on passed hevynesse*
> *That ye han felt, and on the adversite*
> *Of other folk, and thynketh how that ye*
> *Han felt that love dorste yow displese,*
> *Or ye han wonne hym with to grete an ese.*

The improvement is unmistakable, but no one would claim that the revision was primarily for the sake of meter. Throughout this Proem there are many variants but few which can safely be certified as made for metrical reasons. Perhaps one in i. 2 where for *the kyng* α has merely *kyng,* making a nine-syllable line. There is a peculiar variant in 1. 20. Skeat and Robinson have *To any lovere,* which is the reading of α and of CpH3CxTh, and makes easy meter; but the rest have *Unto any lovere* (followed by Root), which makes a needless difficulty: either an extra syllable or a forced elision (Globe prints *Unt'*). If α had it right and the good γ MS Cp, why the change? It could be of course scribal vagary; or it could be that Chaucer, having removed *Unto* in 1 13, really wanted it here, regardless of conventional meter. L. 78 was a good nine-syllable line in α:

> *Wherfor to departe al softely,*   178

which seems to have been weakened with *For which, for to.* Similarly, in 1 147 α has *whoso kan,* the rest *whoso that kan.* In 1 87 the γ mss have

> *That Calkas traitor fals fled was and allied.*

The rest omit *fals* (cf. *falsly* 89, *fals* 93); γ can hardly be Chaucer's. In 1 164 γ has *Palladion the service* (so Skeat and Robinson); αβ omit *the* (so Globe and Root), but again the omission is more likely to be scribal than authorial. In 1 395 α has

> *But eke save þat (in) our spech is (be) differens,*

which later became

> *But pleinly, save our tonges difference,*

which is an obvious improvement, but if Chaucer wanted simply to improve the meter he could have just omitted *eke.*

And so on and on. There is no need to accumulate further evidence of this sort. Nowhere in the recorded variants can one find any alterations which can be regarded as made by Chaucer solely, or even primarily, for the sake of the meter.

The whole matter of these 'revisions,' not only in the α MS as against βγ, but particularly the differences between β and γ, needs further study. Root, who was most familiar with it, reached only very general conclusions: revision for artistic reasons. It is clear from the three considerable additions to α that Chaucer at one time went back to his first version and reviewed it. It is not so clear, however, that two of the additions, namely, the soliloquy on free will and the *Teseida* stanzas, are artistic improvements. For the rest, it would be a plausible hypothesis that many of the apparent alterations were necessitated by Adam's *negligence and rape*; many more may not be revisions at all but the result of inevitable scribal *negligence* or possible shop 'editing' such as Manly postulated in the text of *CT*. To separate and distinguish these now is scarcely possible; only a very bold man would attempt to do so. There are signs moreover that Book v never received the poet's final critical attention.

INDEX

INDEX OF NAMES